fair isle
TUNISIAN CROCHET

fair isle
TUNISIAN CROCHET

Brenda Bourg

STACKPOLE
BOOKS

Published by
STACKPOLE BOOKS
4501 Forbes Boulevard, Suite 200
Lanham, Maryland 20706
www.stackpolebooks.com

Distributed by NATIONAL BOOK NETWORK

Cover design by Caroline M. Stover
Photography by AJ Bourg and Adam Bourg
Charts created by Laurie Bliss

Library of Congress Cataloging-in-Publication Data

Bourg, Brenda, author.
  Fair isle Tunisian crochet : step-by-step instructions and 16 colorful cowls, sweaters, and more / Brenda Bourg.
    pages cm
  ISBN 978-0-8117-1538-6

1. Crocheting—Patterns. 2. Dress accessories. I. Title.

TT825.B6565 2016
746.43'4—dc23

                              2015027183

Printed in India

Contents

Acknowledgments

To my husband, Robert, thank you for your encouragement and support. Without you there would be no book. Thank you for answering every "What if?" with "Have faith!" and for every time I said, "I can't" you replied, "You'll get it!" You've endured countless frozen leftover meals, hurriedly thrown together just so I could do one more row. You've only mildly complained about the laundry mountain that has grown while I was so preoccupied. You've even endured an empty fridge a time or two. You are the love of my life and I thank you for all you've encouraged and empowered me to do. Thank you feels so inadequate.

To my sons, AJ Bourg and Adam Bourg, and daughter-in-law, Christin Bourg, your photography and modeling helped make mom's dream come true! I love you with all my heart and am so grateful for all the time and talent you gave to make it happen. Thank you.

To my sister, Laurie Bliss, thank you for making all my charts! You are an awesome sister and I love you very much!

To my brother, Paul Andrew, thank you for your confidence in me and endless encouragement. I am so thankful for you and love you very much!

To the rest of my family, I love you all and am so grateful for your support!

Tammy Hildebrand, you are my forever mentor! I am so blessed to have you in my corner, and I appreciate your hard-earned wisdom and sound advice. Thank you for always making time for me; I don't know what I'd do without you! I truly value our friendship!

Cindy Fiebig, you have such a God-given talent for tech editing! Thank you for all your hard work. I really appreciate all that you do.

Cindy Geile, Lori Ridgway, Belinda Weldon, Andee Graves, April Garwood, Renee Rodgers, Bendy Carter, Ellen Gormely, Kim Guzman, Deb Seda-Testut, Nancy Smith, Linda Dean, Susan Lowman, Karen Whooley, Karen McKenna, Amy Shelton, Donna Hulka, Bonnie Barker, Joycelyn Sass, Bonnie Pierce, Sara Meyer, Carol Alexander, and Margaret Hubert, you ladies rock! Thank you for your encouragement and friendship. You are all a very special part of my life and I am truly grateful for each of you!

To Mark Allison, Candi Derr, and Stackpole Books, thank you for all your hard work and for giving me the opportunity to make my dream come true!

To you, dear reader, thank you for buying my book! Without you there would be no book!

And most of all, I would like to thank the Lord for my talent and the opportunities He's given me to use them. With Him all things have become possible! "For I know the plans I have for you," declares the Lord, "plans to prosper you and not to harm you, plans to give you hope and a future."—Jeremiah 29:11

Introduction

Have you ever longingly admired Fair Isle patterns and lamented that you couldn't knit? Or maybe you are like me and you just really enjoy Tunisian crochet more—even if you do knit.

I love the traditional snowflake designs; they are what drew me to Fair Isle, in any form, to begin with. The high contrast between light and dark is mesmerizing, and they bring to my mind winter, warmth, and home—all things comfortable and cozy. Some of my favorite sweaters, that I probably should have let go of long ago, are in Fair Isle. While I no longer wear them, they still serve as lovely reminders of how beautiful Fair Isle is, even when worn and tattered by time.

I was incredibly fortunate to stumble across this Fair Isle technique while swatching a Tunisian crochet stitch for a design for another book. I couldn't wait to finish that design so I could play with this concept even more. It wasn't long before I found that everything I wanted to knit in Fair Isle I could do in Tunisian crochet. That was huge for me! I am a much faster and more proficient crocheter than knitter. The afghans that would have taken me months to knit now only took weeks in Tunisian crochet. I can also use any Fair Isle chart I want!

Thankfully, since the front of the project is always facing me I have found I am less likely to miss a stitch in the chart using Tunisian crochet. That's a very big bonus for me. I tend to have to rip out my knitting frequently when working on charts. Amazingly, that rarely happens with this technique.

If you've done much Tunisian crochet, you've probably learned the Tunisian knit stitch. It's a versatile stitch that really does look just like knitting. All of the Fair Isle designs in this book were created using the Tunisian knit stitch. I've found that it creates the crispest look, and it is hard to tell the difference between Fair Isle knitting and Fair Isle Tunisian crochet from the right side of the item. The main difference would be in the bulkiness of the project. Tunisian crochet will always be much thicker and, of course, heavier. What is accomplished in one row of knitting requires a forward and return pass in Tunisian crochet.

Sweaters can be made in Fair Isle Tunisian crochet—there are two included in this book. The yarns must be lighter, and the bulkiness must be factored into the design. Fair Isle Tunisian crochet is also thicker than regular Tunisian crochet because you are carrying two or more unworked yarns behind the project. In some cases you need to lock the floats due to the long carries—I cover that technique a bit later in the book. The bulkiness can make a very cozy sweater that's perfect for cold winter days.

For these Fair Isle patterns we will be using a Tunisian crochet hook with a long cable attached to it. I used Knitter's Pride Dreamz Tunisian/Afghan Hook Set, but the Denise Interchangeable Crochet Hook Set would work beautifully too. You really do need the long cables for the majority of the projects in this book. They will be an investment you won't regret. The cable will allow you to stretch your project out and "read" your work as you go along. Being able to look back over the last few rows will help keep mistakes to a minimum. It's also very inspiring to stretch out your work and watch the pattern unfold as you crochet! It's a great incentive to keep you going "just one more row" too!

The charts may seem a bit intimidating to begin with, but please don't let that stop you from trying Fair Isle Tunisian crochet. After reading my advice on how to work the charts—and a bit of practice—you will be able to make all of these projects. The afghans do look a bit daunting, but they are actually very easy once you understand the charts. You could even make them after you have made the headbands and cowls. They truly are that easy, and they really do work up quickly.

For this book I kept the color selection fairly simple. When first learning Fair Isle, it's best to only use two colors. It makes it easier to learn your own rhythm for managing multiple skeins. Once you feel comfortable with two skeins, you may want to add more colors for a truly fantastic Fair Isle pattern. An easy Fair Isle stitch can really come alive with several colors. Play around with the ones I've used, but don't be afraid to swap out for your favorite colors. I've included an in-depth section on color. Once you've learned your yarn-management rhythm, I hope you use that information to choose some truly spectacular color combinations of your own.

You will read the words "tension," "gauge," and "block" repeatedly throughout my instructions. They are incredibly important if you want to achieve the look I did. It is particularly easy to get off course in Fair Isle Tunisian crochet in these areas. Tension can really tighten, and gauge can go way off course when you start working on your chart, which is why I've included them and stressed them multiple times—I learned the hard way. I'd like to spare you that experience and share my hard-earned wisdom with you.

I really hope this book is just a jumping-off point for many of you. There are so many great charts out there—I would love to see them turned into afghans, headbands, cowls, sweaters, and more using Fair Isle Tunisian crochet. I hope this technique brings you as many hours of enjoyment as it has me. If the colors in my designs don't appeal to you, use ones you love. Don't be afraid to swap any of them out and play with the changes. That's what makes it your project! You have the freedom to choose whatever appeals to you!

All About Fair Isle Tunisian Crochet

Please read through these first few pages to get a feel for the technique. I've included helpful advice for every step of the project—from beginning to end! Please don't skip reading any of the information. It's pretty easy reading and will make the technique move along quickly for you. Once you get started, you will soon realize that it's not a hard technique, but I have covered many things to help keep the frustration level down for a beginner.

Fair Isle Tunisian Crochet

Fair Isle knitting is named for a tiny island in the north of Scotland, which forms part of the Shetland Islands. In the beginning the name referred to knitting that only had two colors per row, but in time, it grew to include the use of many colors per row.

Tunisian crochet is also known as afghan stitch or shepherd's knitting. Tunisian crochet is worked with a very long crochet hook or on a crochet hook that has a cable you attach to it. It creates a very dense fabric that is perfect for cold-weather items. The ends do tend to curl the most in the Tunisian knit stitch so you want to be sure to read about blocking your project. It is a highly necessary step in order to have a beautifully finished project.

No matter which stitch you use, Tunisian crochet is always worked in two passes: the forward pass and the return pass. There are many different varieties of

the forward pass, but the return pass is usually worked the same every time. Each "row" is considered both forward and return pass. Each row of the charts, in this book, is one row of Tunisian crochet.

Fair Isle Tunisian crochet is a beautiful combination of color and the Tunisian knit stitch. You will be working with two or more colors per row. After reading through the following chapters you will understand how to read the chart, pull up your new color, lock your floats, and manage your yarns so you have a professional finish to the project you've invested so much time in. We will even cover how to have the woven backing that is so coveted by knitters!

Once your project is finished, we will go over how to professionally block and seam your work. These steps ensure that you have a quality item when you finish.

Yarn and Yarn Substitution

While I've used all nonwool fibers in this book, you are more than welcome to use wool if you are able to. Wool traditionally is the fiber of choice with Fair Isle simply because the "floats" tend to grab onto each other and naturally felt together on the backside over time. What is a float? It's the unused yarn that is carried on the back of the project. Felting can be a nice little feature that helps get rid of the small loops that occur and are so easily snagged on!

If you are going to substitute the yarns called for in this book, you are going to need to swatch! No skipping it! Not all yarns listed in the same weight are the same weight. For example, some worsted weights are a very thin worsted weight, while others can be a very thick worsted weight. The only way to tell if your substitution will work is to do the swatch. It will be time very well spent, trust me!

Once you have made your swatch, you need to block it. Stitches can really relax when you block them, depending on your yarn, so don't skip this part, as tempting as it may be. Let your swatch fully dry, too. You can only get accurate measurements on a completely dry swatch.

Now that your swatch has dried, measure it. Did you get my gauge? If not, you will need to go with a different hook size or a different yarn. Continue to play with the hook and yarn changes until you are satisfied. This is your project; you need to be happy with the results.

Once you have swatched and chosen the yarn you want to use as substitute, you will have to calculate the yardage you will need. The most accurate measurement for calculating the yarn needed for your substitution is yards. Start by calculating the total yardage needed for each color in your pattern. To do that, look at the number of skeins the pattern calls for in each color and the amount of yardage each skein has. Multiply the yardage of one skein by the total number of skeins of each color. Now you have the total yardage needed for each color.

After calculating the total yardage needed for each color, divide that number by the yards in one skein of your substitution yarn. That will give you the total number of skeins needed for each color in the project. I usually round up one more skein to be safe, unless it's a small project.

All that said, don't be afraid to try! It's always a learning process—and that's my favorite part of the fiber arts! There are no mistakes or failures—just opportunities to learn how the fiber we love so much works, or in some cases, doesn't work.

Stitches Tutorial

Fair Isle Tunisian crochet is simply the introduction of charts to the Tunisian knit stitch. With these easy-to-follow photo tutorials and a little practice you will be off and Fair Isle stitching in no time!

Foundation Row

1. Insert hook in second chain from hook.

2. Yarn over.

3. Pull up loop.

4. *Insert hook in next chain.

5. Yarn over.

6. Pull up loop, repeat from * across. Leave all loops on hook. Do not turn.

Return Pass

1. Yarn over.

2. Pull through 1 loop on hook.

3. *Yarn over.

4. Pull through 2 loops on hook.

5. Repeat from * across until 1 loop remains.

Tunisian Knit Stitch (TKS)

1. Skip first vertical bar, *insert hook through next stitch from front to back between strands of vertical bar.

2. Yarn over.

3. Pull up a loop.

4. Repeat from * across until 1 stitch remains.

5. Insert hook through both loops in end stitch.

6. Yarn over.

(continued)

7. Pull up loop. Do not turn.

Return Pass

1. Yarn over.

2. Pull through 1 loop on hook.

3. *Yarn over.

4. Pull through 2 loops on hook.

5. Repeat from * across until 1 loop remains. Do not turn.

Tunisian Purl Stitch (TPS)

1. Skip first vertical bar, bring yarn in front of work.

2. *Insert hook under next vertical bar.

3. Yarn over.

4. Pull up a loop.

5. Repeat from * across until 1 stitch remains. Insert hook through both loops in end stitch.

6. Yarn over.

(continued)

7. Pull loop up. Do not turn.

Return Pass

1. Yarn over.

2. Pull through 1 loop.

3. *Yarn over.

4. Pull through 2 loops on hook.

5. Repeat from * across until 1 loop remains.

Tunisian Increase Stitch

Insert hook between stitches indicated, yarn over, pull up loop, increase made.

Tunisian Seed Stitch

Repeat Rows 1 and 2 for Tunisian seed stitch.

Row 1

1. Skip first vertical bar, *Tunisian knit stitch in next stitch.

2. Tunisian purl stitch in next stitch. Repeat from * across until 1 stitch remains.

3. *Insert hook through both loops in end stitch.

4. Yarn over.

5. Pull loop up. Do not turn.

RETURN PASS

1. Yarn over.

2. Pull through 1 loop on hook.

3. *Yarn over.

4. Pull through 2 loops on hook.

5. Repeat from * across until 1 loop remains.

Row 2

1. *Tunisian purl stitch in next stitch.

2. Tunisian knit stitch in next stitch.

3. Repeat from * across until 1 stitch remains. Insert hook through both loops in end stitch.

4. Yarn over.

5. Pull loop up. Do not turn.

RETURN PASS

1. Yarn over.

2. Pull through 1 loop.

(continued)

3. *Yarn over.

4. Pull through 2 loops on hook.

5. Repeat from * across until 1 loop remains. Do not turn.

Bind Off

1. Skip first vertical bar. *Insert hook through next stitch from front to back between strands of vertical bar. Yarn over.

2. Pull up loop.

3. Draw yarn through loop on hook. Repeat from * across number of stitches indicated.

Ribbing

Row 1

1. Pull up a loop in color B.

2. Pull up next loop in color A.

3. Repeat across.

RETURN PASS

Work return pass in colors as they are presented.

1. Yarn over and pull through 1 loop on hook.

2. *Yarn over.

3. Pull through 2 loops on hook.

(continued)

4. Repeat from * across until 1 loop remains. Do not turn.

Row 2

1. Skip first vertical bar, *insert hook through next stitch from front to back between strands of vertical bar, with B, yarn over and pull up loop (Tunisian knit stitch made).

2. With A, bring yarn in front of work, insert hook under next vertical bar, yarn over, pull up loop (Tunisian purl stitch made).

3. Repeat from * across until 1 stitch remains. Insert hook through both loops in end stitch.

4. Yarn over.

5. Pull loop up. Do not turn.

RETURN PASS

Work return pass in colors as they are presented.

1. Yarn over.

2. Pull through 1 loop on hook.

3. *Yarn over.

4. Pull through 2 loops on hook.

5. Repeat from * across until 1 loop remains. Do not turn.

Repeat Row 2 for pattern.

Single Crochet

1. Insert hook where pattern instructs and yarn over.

2. Pull through loop.

3. Yarn over.

4. Pull through both loops.

Back Loop Single Crochet

1. Insert hook underneath the back loop only in stitch below.

2. Yarn over.

3. Pull through loop.

4. Yarn over.

5. Pull through both loops.

At first glance charts can seem a bit intimidating, but Tunisian Fair Isle charts are actually relatively simple to follow. Each square represents one Tunisian knit stitch and each chart row represents one row of Fair Isle Tunisian knit stitch. The forward and return pass are always considered one row. Each chart is colored according to the colors of the pattern.

Fair Isle charts, regardless whether knit or Tunisian crochet, are always read from bottom to top and right to left. In Fair Isle Tunisian crochet every row is started on the right side of the chart. This method makes it really easy to stay on top of your place in the chart! No missed stitches or dropped colors!

In Fair Isle Tunisian crochet you will always work the return pass stitch in the same color you worked the forward pass stitch.

For ease of following the Fair Isle chart, always mark the beginning of every row of your chart. Another way of tracking which row to work is to highlight every other row. Using sticky notes can also help keep track of what row you are working in the chart. Just move the sticky note up on the chart as you complete the row.

Using stitch markers to mark the beginning of each pattern repeat also cuts down on any confusion, especially at the very beginning of the Fair Isle chart pattern. Be sure to only use locking markers—you want to be able to open and close them in order to move them up your work.

With a bit of practice, chart reading will come naturally and without much thought.

Working with Multiple Colors and Changing Colors

Working with more than one color can very easily turn into a tangled mess! The best way to avoid that is to hold each yarn in a different hand. I like to keep one ball on my right side and the second on my left. The odds of ending up with a giant knot become much lower with this method. When working with three or more colors, it does become a bit more challenging, but it is manageable once you get your own system worked out. You can use yarn jars, separate bags, or even coffee cans with holes cut into the lids to hold your yarns and keep them from getting tangled.

Changing colors can be a challenge when you are first learning Fair Isle Tunisian crochet. When changing color at the beginning of a row, work the yarn over in the new color when two loops remain on the hook at the end of the previous row. Pull the new color through the two loops and begin the next row. This method only works if the first stitch is in the new color.

Start the new color for the next row by working the last yarn over and pull through of the previous row in the new color.

Pull the new color through two loops and you are ready to begin the next row in the new color.

Sometimes, though, the pattern does call for a mid-row color change. To do this we simply drop the first yarn and pull the new yarn through next stitch, leaving a long enough tail for weaving in later, and continue working in pattern.

For a midrow color change, drop the first yarn and pull the new yarn through the next stitch, leaving a long enough tail for weaving in later.

When we finish our forward pass, we need to come back and work each stitch of our return pass in the same color we used in each stitch of the forward pass. In other words, always work the return pass in colors as they are presented.

Locking Carrying Color

Once in a while, long carries of the unused color are unavoidable in Fair Isle Tunisian crochet. Most patterns try to keep the carries to only four or five stitches, but sometimes that's just not possible. While your work shouldn't be so loose that you have stretches of yarn that are hanging out and getting easily snagged on, longer unused colors can make that a challenge. The best way to combat that issue is to learn to lock your floats. The float is that bit of unworked yarn that is hanging on the back. Locking floats is a knitting term that is just as applicable to Fair Isle Tunisian crochet.

To lock your float, you simply wrap the unused yarn around the yarn you are working with, about midway through the carry, on the back side of the project.

Wrap the unused yarn around the yarn you are working with, about midway through the carry, on the back side of the project.

By doing this, you close the gap and make your floats much shorter. Be careful not to pull the unused color up into the stitch of the working color. The idea is to lock it in while still hiding it.

The bumps on the back of the Tunisian crochet tend to absorb the float, so you will likely have a much smaller loop hanging on the back of the project, if any at all. The more you practice locking your floats, the easier it becomes and the tidier the back of your work will be. Eventually, you should become so proficient that the back of the work almost appears woven. It makes a very attractive backing, but it does take practice to achieve the look.

It's really easy to dramatically alter your tension while learning to lock your floats. Usually, your gauge will become much tighter if you don't pay attention. Be sure not to pull the yarns too snug while locking them. You want your project to still have drape and movement. Check your gauge every few rows to make sure you are still on target with it. If you aren't, rip back to where you were and start again.

Learning to lock your floats may take a few times or even a few patterns. Be patient with yourself. It's a new technique and it's okay to make mistakes—just keep trying! Eventually, you will get it!

Tension

It's extremely important that you keep your tension loose! If tension isn't loose, the fabric will pull in and pucker unattractively, not to mention that the size of the item will change dramatically as well. Sometimes, you may need to go up several hook sizes just to maintain gauge and to ease a tight tension. Don't worry about using one or even several hooks larger than the pattern calls for. Gauge and tension are far more important than using the same hook I did!

Tension and gauge can drastically change when you start the charts. Pay attention—if you need to go up in hook size to keep the right tension and gauge, don't be afraid to! You won't need to start the whole project over in the new hook size, just go up the needed sizes for the charts and then drop back down to the smaller size once the charts are done.

Before you start the pattern, it's a good idea to work a swatch of the chart. This will familiarize you with the chart, as well as give you a good idea of what your gauge will do once you start working in Fair Isle. Take the time to block your swatch. Sometimes gauge can really change when you block an item, and this will give you an opportunity on a much smaller scale to see what you might need to adjust. Make sure you allow your swatch to completely dry before measuring and unpinning. If your swatch meets the gauge for the pattern, you are good to go! If not, adjust your hook size and rework your swatch. Once you have done these things, and you have met gauge, you can begin your project with the confidence that the project will fit!

Blocking

Blocking is absolutely necessary with Fair Isle Tunisian crochet. There is no way you can skip it and still have a nicely finished project. Blocking should always be done before you seam your project together.

Steam blocking is my favorite way to tame the curl of Fair Isle Tunisian crochet. Tunisian crochet can be one of the hardest fabrics to get to lay flat. None of the projects in this book are done in wool. I can't use animal fibers so all projects are man-made yarns. If you are able to use animal fibers, it will make blocking a bit easier. They do tend to hold their shape when wet, measured, pinned, and dried.

The yarns in this book are a bit more challenging to block. I steam blocked every single one of them. Please read these instructions carefully! I don't want you to melt the item you have spent so many hours creating!

1. Dampen item, gently squeezing out excess water.
2. Place item on a padded ironing board.
3. Place a wet towel on top of curling edge. Smooth the edge as flat as possible with your hand, making sure there are no lumps or wrinkles.
4. Gently place the iron on top of the wet towel. Do not hold it in place for very long. Lift the iron and wet towel and move them down the edge, repeating the process as you go across.
5. When the item has been completely steam blocked, pin it to blocking mat to dry. Carefully measure the item as you are pinning to make sure it is accurately laid out. Place a fan pointing on the item to help it dry faster. Usually, this will take all the curl out, but if it hasn't, repeat blocking.

If you are uncomfortable with steam blocking or are using a yarn that doesn't need such a heavy-handed blocking, you can just wet block the item.

1. Dampen item, gently squeezing out excess water.
2. Lay item out on blocking mats.
3. Carefully measure item and gently tug into necessary shape.
4. Generously pin item to blocking mat.
5. Place a fan to blow across item to speed drying.

Do not unpin the item until it has thoroughly dried. If you take the pins out too early, the curly edges will return by the time your item fully dries. It's well worth the time it takes to wait for the item to dry!

Seaming

Seaming can be a bit tricky in Fair Isle Tunisian crochet. That last row can have lots of gaps in it even if you did finish with the bind-off stitch. The best way to ruin a great project is to have sloppy seams. To avoid those gaps, sew pieces together by placing right sides together, leaving a $1/4$-inch seam allowance, and seaming pieces together with the backstitch. By leaving this allowance, you are working into the fabric where the stitch is tighter. It closes the gaps nicely and leaves you with a beautifully finished project.

Hints and Tips

1. Go up a hook size or two when working the chart if your tension gets tighter as you go. It's very easy to tense up when working on a new technique. Stop and check every few rows to make sure you are still on track. If you aren't, rip back to where your tension is correct and go up a hook size or two.
2. Work into the bottom "bump" of the starting chain. This technique will help somewhat minimize the curling that often occurs with Fair Isle Tunisian crochet.
3. Use stitch markers to separate pattern repeats. The best stitch markers for Fair Isle Tunisian crochet are locking markers, since you need to be able to open and close them. Using markers will make it easier to figure out where you are in the chart. I find that bold-colored markers work best; they are the easiest to see.
4. Leave yourself long enough tails to weave in and be sure to weave your tails into the same color as the tail! You don't want the weave to show because you have accidently woven it into the contrasting color!

5. Use a copy machine to make your charts bigger and effortless to read. This will also allow you to mark the chart without marking in your book. Mark the last row you worked, making it easier to pick up right where you left off.

6. Use your smartphone to take a photo of the chart to enable you to enlarge and read the chart on your phone or tablet. Some tablets may even allow you to mark the rows as you are moving up the chart.

7. Always be generous with pins when blocking. Heavy pinning is absolutely necessary with Fair Isle Tunisian crochet. After spending the time to block your project, you don't want it to curl just because you didn't pin it enough.

8. Check your work every few rows to ensure you haven't made any errors you've missed. Look at each chart repeat to make certain they all look the same. Better to have to rip back just a few rows than most of the project!

9. You never turn your work in Fair Isle Tunisian crochet. The right side should always be facing you.

10. The last stitch on every forward row will always be a Tunisian simple stitch no matter what stitches the pattern used in the rest of the row.

11. Stop and stretch! It is really easy to get hand cramps doing Fair Isle Tunisian crochet—the way we hold the hook really lends itself to that. Fan your fingers out and gently stretch them; next, roll them into a fist, and then gently fan your fingers out again. Repeat this stretch a few times every twenty minutes or so to prevent injury.

12. Stop and count the loops on your hook every few rows. Better to catch a dropped stitch early!

Helpful Tools

Place Markers

Post-it notes are invaluable little helpers to keep you on track in your chart. You could also use a magnetic or clear ruler to help keep your place.

Stitch Markers

Locking stitch markers work best with any Fair Isle Tunisian crochet project. You need to be able to open and close them to move them up the rows of your project. They are a wonderful way to help split up the chart repeat so you know exactly where the beginning and end stitches are. Using different color markers makes it even easier to spot exactly where you are in your chart.

Tape Measure

You can never have too many tape measures! I find a retractable tape measure the best bet for my work bag. It's less likely to get tangled up in my yarn. While working a chart, it really pays to measure every few inches to make sure the work isn't being pulled in too tight.

Scissors

I keep several pairs of scissors in my work bag. Some work better on thicker yarns, others on thinner yarns. Never break your yarn—a cut end is much easier to thread through the yarn needle for weaving in ends.

Yarn Needle

A blunt-tip needle works best for weaving in ends and sewing pieces together. Keep several sizes on hand for the different weights of yarn.

Straight Pins

Pins are an absolute necessity when blocking! I use the ball-head pin. They are colorful, easy to handle, and I am much less likely to miss pulling one out if it has a big bright red top!

Blocking Mats

While you can use towels and a spare bed, exercise mats make wonderful blocking mats! They are very forgiving about being poked with pins and will keep any color that bleeds from reaching your carpet. I have white exercise mats that are easily cleaned and stored when not in use.

Pencil and Paper

These always come in handy if you like to make notes on the pattern you are making. Maybe you would like to change the row count a bit to make the item more custom? Keeping notes is the best way to ensure you will be able to repeat any changes you've made to make the project uniquely yours!

Choosing Your Own Colors

Do you need a little help picking your own colors for each project? Maybe you are ready to add more than two colors to the project. Choosing colors can be very intimidating. You want the Fair Isle to pop but not in a garish way.

My favorite way to choose coordinating yarn is to base the colors on my stash of variegated yarn that I have collected over the years. First, this really shows me what colors I am attracted to. Naturally we tend to gravitate toward the color schemes we love. What better way to choose a color combination? Secondly, I know those colors will work together because they already do in skeins I have.

The biggest downfall with this method is that sometimes the colors match too closely for a particular Fair Isle chart. You lose the color change and it becomes bland. I have found that moving up or down a shade in the same color can correct that. Suddenly, the pattern really sings!

Another option is to use a color wheel. There are several different ways to use the wheel to choose the colors for your project. Each way has its own merit— the method you choose really depends on the look you want your finished Fair Isle project to have.

Complementary Colors

Complementary colors are the colors that are directly across from each other on the color wheel. They will be highly contrasting colors and create a very dramatic effect that can be quite lovely.

Split Complementary Colors

Split complementary colors are one over from the opposite color on the color wheel. To find this, pick your first color, look across the wheel and find its complementary color, then select the two colors on either side of the complementary color. This creates a harmonious Fair Isle Tunisian crochet pattern that is very pleasing to the eye!

Primary Colors

Primary colors are the basic colors of red, blue, and yellow. They are highly contrasting colors that can create a very bright and beautiful Fair Isle Tunisian crochet pattern.

Secondary Colors

Secondary colors are created by mixing primary colors—think orange, green, and purple. They are very complementary to primary colors and can create a lovely gradient Fair Isle Tunisian crochet pattern when combined with primary colors.

Analogous Colors

Analogous colors are right next to each other on the color wheel. They look pleasant together because they are closely related. These color schemes are the ones we most often see in nature. These usually create a bit more subdued Fair Isle Tunisian crochet pattern.

Triadic Colors

Triadic colors are colors that are evenly spaced around the color wheel. These combinations tend to be dramatic, even if you use pale or unsaturated versions of your colors. For color harmony, choose

Color Wheel

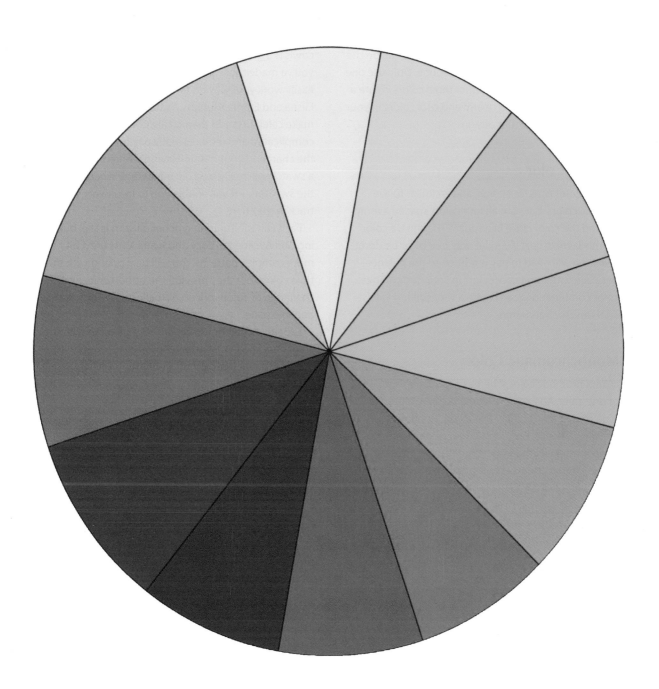

only one color to dominate and use the two others for a natural balance.

Tetradic Color

Tetradic colors use four colors arranged into two complementary pairs—imagine placing a rectangle on the color wheel to make your color selection. Only use one dominant color and let the other three colors create a natural balance between warm and cool colors in your Fair Isle Tunisian crochet design.

Square Color

Square color uses four colors and is similar to the tetradic colors, but with all four colors spaced evenly around the color circle in a square. The square color method works best if you let only one color be dominant. You will need to pay attention to the balance between warm and cool colors in your design. These color combinations can create a very striking Fair Isle Tunisian crochet design.

Monochromatic Color

Monochromatic color schemes use varying shades of one color. An example would be baby blue, ocean blue, and midnight blue. These combinations can create very pleasing Fair Isle Tunisian crochet patterns.

No matter which method you use to choose your colors, all that counts is that you love the colors you are working with. You really need to be happy with your choice—it makes learning a new technique much easier if you are excited about what you see coming alive at the end of your hook!

When first learning Fair Isle Tunisian crochet, it's best to start with a smaller project. Most of the projects in this book are geared toward the beginner. Starting with the headbands and working your way up to the cowls is a great introduction to the technique. Once you've made those projects, you should be able to easily work your way on to the Annabel Bag or the Elisha and Emma Afghans. As for the sweaters, I would make Laleh first and then tackle Cora. Cora is more complicated and requires really paying attention to the chart and your gauge. Having worked the chart in a swatch will really be a big advantage when making the sweaters—it will enable you to intuitively stay on track in the chart.

Each Fair Isle Tunisian crochet pattern is skill building. The Aveline Jar Cozy and Ivana Mitts are a bit more complex patterns. You will be working with multiple colors, but they provide the opportunity and challenge of colorwork on a smaller and more manageable scale.

Experiment with your favorite colors or go with the colors I've chosen. Whichever project you start with, above all, have fun!

Projects

Adanna Boot Cuffs

Boot cuffs are the perfect accessory to pull a fall outfit together. The Adanna cuffs are lovely with a simple pair of jeans, or you could dress them up with tights and a skirt. In just an afternoon, you can have a lovely addition to your wardrobe!

Skill Level
Beginner

Finished Measurements
$4^1/_2$ in. (11.5 cm) wide x 12 in. (30.5 cm) long

Yarn
Berroco Comfort (50% nylon, 50% acrylic; 3.5 oz./100 g; 210 yd./193 m)
- 2 skeins #9720 Hummus (A)
- 2 skeins #9703 Barley (B)

Hook & Other Materials
- US I/9 (5.5 mm) Tunisian crochet cabled hook or size to obtain gauge
- Yarn needle
- Stitch markers

Gauge
In TKS 17 sts and 16 rows = 4 in. (10 cm)

Pattern Stitches

Foundation Row: Insert hook in second chain from hook, yarn over, pull up loop, *insert hook in next chain, yarn over, pull up loop; repeat from * across. Leave all loops on hook. Do not turn. **Return Pass:** Yarn over, pull through 1 loop on hook,*yarn over, pull through 2 loops on hook; repeat from * across until 1 loop remains. (See step-by-step instructions on page 3.)

Tunisian Purl Stitch (TPS): Skip first vertical bar, bring yarn in front of work,*insert hook under next vertical bar, yarn over, pull up loop; repeat from * across until 1 stitch remains, insert hook through both loops in end stitch, yarn over, pull loop up. Do not turn. **Return Pass:** Yarn over, pull through 1 loop, *yarn over, pull through 2 loops on hook; repeat from * across until 1 loop remains. (See step-by-step instructions on page 7.)

Tunisian Knit Stitch (TKS): Skip first vertical bar, *insert hook through next stitch from front to back between strands of vertical bar, yarn over, pull up loop; repeat from * across until 1 stitch remains, insert hook through both loops in end stitch, yarn over, pull loop up. Do not turn. **Return Pass:** Yarn over, pull through 1 loop on hook, *yarn over, pull through 2 loops on hook; repeat from * across until 1 loop remains. Do not turn. (See step-by-step instructions on page 5.)

Bind Off: Skip first vertical bar, *insert hook through next stitch from front to back between strands of vertical bar, yarn over, pull up loop, draw yarn through loop on hook; repeat from * across number of stitches indicated. (See step-by-step instructions on page 12.)

Notes

If gauge pulls in too tight when working chart, go up a hook size or two. Do not pull yarns tight while working—it will cause puckering in the fabric and distortion of the pattern.

Instructions (make two)

With A, loosely ch 50.

Row 1 (RS): Work Foundation Row across.

Rows 2–3: Work TPS in each st across.

Row 4: Work TKS in each st across.

Rows 5–14: With A and B, work Chart in TKS in each st across.

Fasten off B.

Row 15: With A, work TKS in each st across.

Rows 16–17: Work TPS in each st across.

Bind off. Fasten off.

Finishing

With yarn needle, weave in tails. Dampen cuffs, gently squeezing out excess water. Place cuffs on a padded ironing board. Place a wet towel on top of curling edge. Smooth the edge as flat as possible with your hand, making sure there are no lumps or wrinkles. Gently place the iron on top of the wet towel. Do not hold it in place for very long. Lift the iron and wet towel and move down the edge, repeating the process as you go across. When cuffs have been completely steam blocked, pin to blocking mat and allow to fully dry. Sew ends together.

Adanna Boot Cuffs

Color A

Color B

Hanna Boot Cuffs

Hanna will bring any outfit alive with just the right punch of color! These boot cuffs are easy to make and can be whipped up in just a day or two.

Skill Level
Beginner

Finished Measurements
6 in. (15 cm) wide x 12 in. (28 cm) long

Yarn
Universal Yarn Bamboo Pop (50% cotton, 50% bamboo; 3.5 oz./100 g;
    292 yd./267 m)
- 2 skeins #104 Rose (A)
- 2 skeins #110 Sand (B)

Hook & Other Materials
- US I/9 (5.5 mm) Tunisian crochet cabled hook or size to obtain gauge
- Yarn needle
- Stitch markers

Gauge
In TKS 20 sts and 20 rows = 4 in. (10 cm)

Pattern Stitches

Foundation Row: Insert hook in second chain from hook, yarn over, pull up loop, *insert hook in next chain, yarn over, pull up loop; repeat from * across. Leave all loops on hook. Do not turn. **Return Pass:** Yarn over, pull through 1 loop on hook, *yarn over, pull through 2 loops on hook; repeat from * across until 1 loop remains. (See step-by-step instructions on page 3.)

Tunisian Purl Stitch (TPS): Skip first vertical bar, bring yarn in front of work,*insert hook under next vertical bar, yarn over, pull up loop; repeat from * across until 1 stitch remains, insert hook through both loops in end stitch, yarn over, pull loop up. Do not turn. **Return Pass:** Yarn over, pull through 1 loop, *yarn over, pull through 2 loops on hook; repeat from * across until 1 loop remains. (See step-by-step instructions on page 7.)

Tunisian Knit Stitch (TKS): Skip first vertical bar, *insert hook through next stitch from front to back between strands of vertical bar, yarn over, pull up loop; repeat from * across until 1 stitch remains, insert hook through both loops in end stitch, yarn over, pull loop up. Do not turn. **Return Pass:** Yarn over, pull through 1 loop on hook, *yarn over, pull through 2 loops on hook; repeat from * across until 1 loop remains. Do not turn. (See step-by-step instructions on page 5.)

Bind Off: Skip first vertical bar, *insert hook through next stitch from front to back between strands of vertical bar, yarn over, pull up loop, draw yarn through loop on hook; repeat from * across number of stitches indicated. (See step-by-step instructions on page 12.)

Notes

- Bamboo has little flexibility so you really need to stay on top of your tension!
- Remember, if your gauge pulls in too tight when working the chart, go up a hook size or two. Also, do not pull yarns tight while working—it will cause puckering in the fabric and distortion of the pattern.

Instructions (make two)

With A, loosely ch 60.
Row 1 (RS): Work Foundation Row across.
Rows 2–3: Work TPS in each st across.
Rows 4–26: With A and B, work Chart in TKS in each st across.
Fasten off B.
Rows 27–28: With A, work TPS in each st across.
Bind off.
Fasten off.

Finishing

With yarn needle, weave in tails. Dampen boot cuffs, gently squeezing out any excess water. Place cuffs on a padded ironing board. Place a wet towel on top of curling edge. Smooth the edge as flat as possible with your hand, making sure there are no lumps or wrinkles. Gently place the iron on top of the wet towel. Do not hold it in place for very long. Lift the iron and wet towel and move down the edge, repeating the process as you go across. When cuffs have been completely steam blocked, pin to blocking mat and allow to fully dry. Sew ends together.

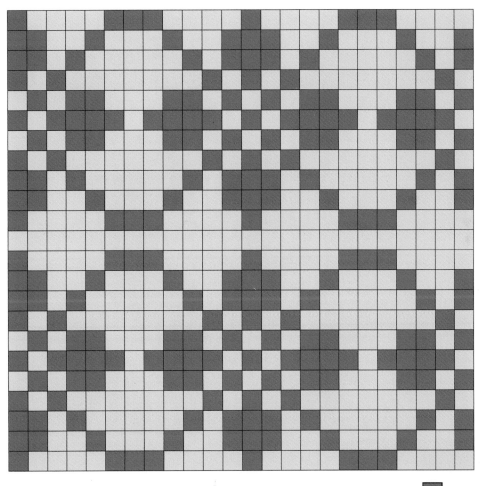

Hanna Boot Cuffs

■ Color A
□ Color B

Aveline Jar Cozy

Aveline is a vibrant way to brighten a work desk or corner table! This pattern is a bit more advanced. You are working with several colors, but the outcome is well worth the effort!

Skill Level
Intermediate

Finished Measurements
About $4^1/_2$ in. (11.5 cm) wide x 10 in. (25.5 cm) long

Yarn
Universal Yarn Bamboo Pop (50% cotton, 50% bamboo; 3.5 oz./100 g; 292 yd./267 m)
- 1 skein #109 Clover (A)
- 1 skein #102 Cream (B)
- 1 skein #214 Sunsetter (C)
- 1 skein #115 Silken (D)

Hook & Other Materials
- US I/9 (5.5 mm) Tunisian crochet cabled hook or size to obtain gauge
- Yarn needle
- Stitch markers

Gauge
Gauge is not critical.

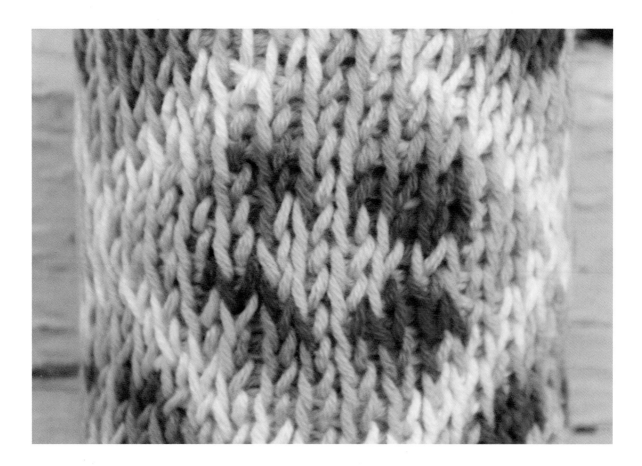

Pattern Stitches

Foundation Row: Insert hook in second chain from hook, yarn over, pull up loop, *insert hook in next chain, yarn over, pull up loop; repeat from * across. Leave all loops on hook. Do not turn. **Return Pass:** Yarn over, pull through 1 loop on hook, *yarn over, pull through 2 loops on hook; repeat from * across until 1 loop remains. (See step-by-step instructions on page 3.)

Tunisian Purl Stitch (TPS): Skip first vertical bar, bring yarn in front of work,*insert hook under next vertical bar, yarn over, pull up loop; repeat from * across until 1 stitch remains, insert hook through both loops in end stitch, yarn over, pull loop up. Do not turn. **Return Pass:** Yarn over, pull through 1 loop, *yarn over, pull through 2 loops on hook; repeat from * across until 1 loop remains. (See step-by-step instructions on page 7.)

Tunisian Knit Stitch (TKS): Skip first vertical bar, *insert hook through next stitch from front to back between strands of vertical bar, yarn over, pull up loop; repeat from * across until 1 stitch remains, insert hook through both loops in end stitch, yarn over, pull loop up. Do not turn. **Return Pass:** Yarn over, pull through 1 loop on hook, *yarn over, pull through 2 loops on hook; repeat from * across until 1 loop remains. Do not turn. (See step-by-step instructions on page 5.)

Bind Off: Skip first vertical bar, *insert hook through next stitch from front to back between strands of vertical bar, yarn over, pull up loop, draw yarn through loop on hook; repeat from * across number of stitches indicated. (See step-by-step instructions on page 12.)

Notes

If gauge pulls in too tight when working chart, go up a hook size or two. Do not pull yarns tight while working—it will cause puckering in the fabric and distortion of the pattern.

Instructions

With A, loosely ch 42.

Row 1 (RS): Work Foundation Row across.

Rows 2–3: Work TPS in each st across.

Row 4: Work TKS in each st across.

Rows 5–19: With A, B, C, and D, work Chart in TKS in each st across.

Fasten off B, C, and D.

Row 20: With A, work TKS in each st across.

Rows 21–22: Work TPS in each st across.

Bind off.

Fasten off.

Finishing

With yarn needle, weave in tails. Dampen jar cozy, gently squeezing out excess water. Place jar cozy on a padded ironing board. Place a wet towel on top of curling edge. Smooth the edge as flat as possible with your hand, making sure there are no lumps or wrinkles. Gently place the iron on top of the wet towel. Do not hold it in place for very long. Lift the iron and wet towel and move down the edge, repeating the process as you go across. When jar cozy has been completely steam blocked, pin to blocking mat and allow to fully dry. Sew ends together.

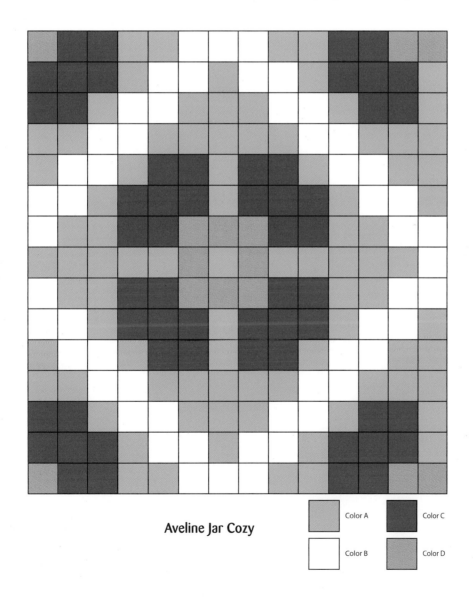

Aveline Jar Cozy

	Color A		Color C
	Color B		Color D

Annabel Bag

Annabel gives the subtle illusion of working with multiple yarns, while only using two. It's the perfect project bag! The colors are inspiring and the size is big enough to hold even your largest WIPS (works-in-progress)!

Skill Level
Intermediate

Finished Measurements
Each body: about 16 in. (38 cm) wide x 14^1/$_2$ in. (38 cm) long
Side strip: about 5 in. (13 cm) wide x 45 in. (114 cm) long

Yarn
Red Heart Super Saver (100% acrylic; 7 oz./198 g; 364 yd./333 m)
• 3 skeins #0312 Black (A)
Red Heart Boutique Unforgettable (100% acrylic; 3.5 oz./100 g; 269 yd./246 m)
• 3 skeins #3955 Winery (B)

Hook & Other Materials
• US J/10 (6.0 mm) Tunisian crochet cabled hook or size to obtain gauge
• 10 in. wooden handles
• Fabric for lining bag
• Yarn needle
• Stitch markers

Gauge
In TKS 14 sts and 14 rows = 4 in. (10 cm)

vertical bar, yarn over, pull up loop, draw yarn through loop on hook; repeat from * across number of stitches indicated. (See step-by-step instructions on page 12.)

Notes
- The side panel of the bag is made in one long strip.
- If gauge pulls in too tight when working chart, go up a hook size or two. Do not pull yarns tight while working—it will cause puckering in the fabric and distortion of the pattern.

Instructions

Body (make two)
With A, loosely ch 55.

Row 1 (RS): Work Foundation Row across.

Rows 2–3: Work TKS in each st across.

Rows 4–48: With A, TKS in each of next 3 sts, *with A and B, work Chart in TKS in each st across, with A, TKS in each of next 3 sts; repeat from * across.

Note: On the last repeat of the chart, you do not work the top 3 rows.

Fasten off B.

Rows 49–51: With A, work TKS in each st across.

Fasten off.

Side Panel
With A, loosely ch 23.

Row 1 (RS): Work Foundation Row across.

Rows 2–3: Work TKS in each st across.

Rows 4–144: With A, TKS in each of next 3 sts, with A and B, work Chart in TKS in each st across, with A, TKS in each of last 3 sts.

Note: On the last repeat of the chart, you do not work the top 3 rows.

Fasten off B.

Rows 145–147: With A, work TKS in each st across.

Fasten off.

Handle Flaps (make two)
Row 1: With A, working on top of body panel, skip first 10 sts, pick up 1 loop for each of the next 35 sts, leave last 10 sts unworked. **Return Pass:** Yarn over, pull through 1 loop on hook, *yarn over, pull

Pattern Stitches

Foundation Row: Insert hook in second chain from hook, yarn over, pull up loop, *insert hook in next chain, yarn over, pull up loop; repeat from * across. Leave all loops on hook. Do not turn. **Return Pass:** Yarn over, pull through 1 loop on hook, *yarn over, pull through 2 loops on hook; repeat from * across until 1 loop remains. (See step-by-step instructions on page 3.)

Tunisian Knit Stitch (TKS): Skip first vertical bar, *insert hook through next stitch from front to back between strands of vertical bar, yarn over, pull up loop; repeat from * across until 1 stitch remains, insert hook through both loops in end stitch, yarn over, pull loop up. Do not turn. **Return Pass:** Yarn over, pull through 1 loop on hook, *yarn over, pull through 2 loops on hook; repeat from * across until 1 loop remains. Do not turn. (See step-by-step instructions on page 5.)

Bind Off: Skip first vertical bar, *insert hook through next stitch from front to back between strands of

through 2 loops on hook; repeat from * across until 1 loop remains. Do not turn.

Rows 2–5: Work TKS in each st across.

Bind off.

Fasten off.

Finishing

With yarn needle, weave in tails. Dampen all bag pieces, gently squeezing out excess water. Place pieces on a padded ironing board. Place a wet towel on top of curling edge. Smooth the edge as flat as possible with your hand, making sure there are no lumps or wrinkles. Gently place the iron on top of the wet towel. Do not hold it in place for very long. Lift the iron and wet towel and move down the edge, repeating the process as you go across. When all pieces have been completely steam blocked, pin to blocking mat and allow to fully dry.

Sew body pieces to side panel and sew in lining. Pull handle flaps through wooden handle slots. Sew flaps to the body to hold handle in place.

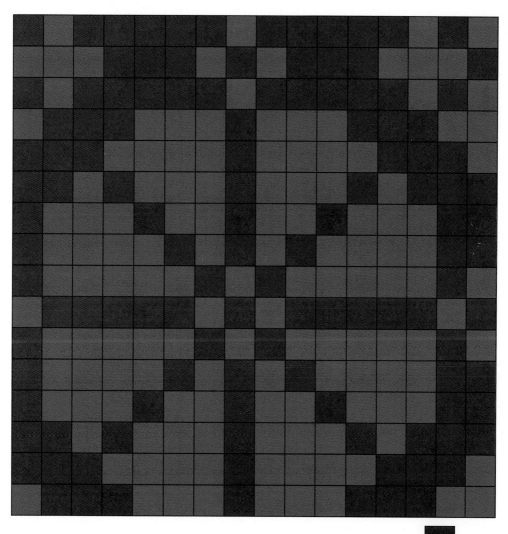

Annabel Bag

Color A

Color B

Reena Headband

Reena is the perfect headband for any snow bunny! It's a very quick project to work up. You could even complete a few in just one day!

Skill Level
Beginner

Finished Measurements
About 3³/₄ in. (8 cm) wide x 20 in. (48 cm) long

Yarn
Universal Yarn Uptown DK (100% acrylic; 3.5 oz./100 g; 273 yd./250 m)
- 1 skein #134 Grenadine (A)
- 1 skein #120 Sahara (B)

Hook & Other Materials
- US H/8 (5 mm) Tunisian crochet cabled hook or size to obtain gauge
- Yarn needle
- Stitch markers

Gauge
In TKS 16 sts and 16 rows = 4 in. (10 cm)

Pattern Stitches

Foundation Row: Insert hook in second chain from hook, yarn over, pull up loop, *insert hook in next chain, yarn over, pull up loop; repeat from * across. Leave all loops on hook. Do not turn. **Return Pass:** Yarn over, pull through 1 loop on hook, *yarn over, pull through 2 loops on hook; repeat from * across until 1 loop remains. (See step-by-step instructions on page 3.)

Tunisian Purl Stitch (TPS): Skip first vertical bar, bring yarn in front of work,*insert hook under next vertical bar, yarn over, pull up loop; repeat from * across until 1 stitch remains, insert hook through both loops in end stitch, yarn over, pull loop up. Do not turn. **Return Pass:** Yarn over, pull through 1 loop, *yarn over, pull through 2 loops on hook; repeat from * across until 1 loop remains. (See step-by-step instructions on page 7.)

Tunisian Knit Stitch (TKS): Skip first vertical bar, *insert hook through next stitch from front to back between strands of vertical bar, yarn over, pull up loop; repeat from * across until 1 stitch remains, insert hook through both loops in end stitch, yarn over, pull loop up. Do not turn. **Return Pass:** Yarn over, pull through 1 loop on hook, *yarn over, pull through 2 loops on hook; repeat from * across until 1 loop remains. Do not turn. (See step-by-step instructions on page 5.)

Bind Off: Skip first vertical bar, *insert hook through next stitch from front to back between strands of vertical bar, yarn over, pull up loop, draw yarn through loop on hook; repeat from * across number of stitches indicated. (See step-by-step instructions on page 12.)

Notes

If gauge pulls in too tight when working chart, go up a hook size or two. Do not pull yarns tight while working—it will cause puckering in the fabric and distortion of the pattern.

Instructions

With A, loosely ch 80.

Row 1 (RS): Work Foundation Row across.

Rows 2–3: Work TPS in each st across.

Row 4: Work TKS in each st across.

Rows 5–11: With A and B, work Chart in TKS in each st across.

Fasten off B.

Row 12: With A, TKS in each st across.

Rows 13–14: Work TPS in each st across.

Bind off.

Fasten off.

Finishing

With yarn needle, weave in tails. Dampen headband, gently squeezing out excess water. Place headband on a padded ironing board. Place a wet towel on top of curling edge. Smooth the edge as flat as possible with your hand, making sure there are no lumps or wrinkles. Gently place the iron on top of the wet towel. Do not hold it in place for very long. Lift the iron and wet towel and move down the edge, repeating the process as you go across. When headband has been completely steam blocked, pin to blocking mat and allow to fully dry. Sew ends together.

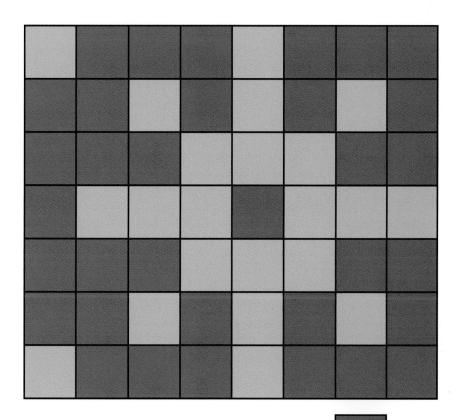

Reena Headband

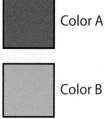

Color A

Color B

Eliza Headband

Eliza is a fun and funky quick project that would be really lovely in a variety of colors!

Skill Level
Beginner

Finished Measurements
About $2^1/_2$ in. (6 cm) wide x 18 in. (53 cm) long

Yarn
Lion Brand Vanna's Choice (100% acrylic; 3.5 oz./100 g; 170 yd./156 m)
- 1 skein #148 Burgundy (A)
- 1 skein #135 Rust (B)

Hook & Other Materials
- US I/9 (5.5 mm) Tunisian crochet cabled hook or size to obtain gauge
- Yarn needle
- Stitch markers

Gauge
In TKS 16 sts and 14 rows = 4 in. (10 cm)

Pattern Stitches

Foundation Row: Insert hook in second chain from hook, yarn over, pull up loop, *insert hook in next chain, yarn over, pull up loop; repeat from * across. Leave all loops on hook. Do not turn. **Return Pass:** Yarn over, pull through 1 loop on hook, *yarn over, pull through 2 loops on hook; repeat from * across until 1 loop remains. (See step-by-step instructions on page 3.)

Tunisian Knit Stitch (TKS): Skip first vertical bar, *insert hook through next stitch from front to back between strands of vertical bar, yarn over, pull up loop; repeat from * across until 1 stitch remains, insert hook through both loops in end stitch, yarn over, pull loop up. Do not turn. **Return Pass:** Yarn over, pull through 1 loop on hook, *yarn over, pull through 2 loops on hook; repeat from * across until 1 loop remains. Do not turn. (See step-by-step instructions on page 5.)

Bind Off: Skip first vertical bar, *insert hook through next stitch from front to back between strands of vertical bar, yarn over, pull up loop, draw yarn through loop on hook; repeat from * across number of stitches indicated. (See step-by-step instructions on page 12.)

Notes

If gauge pulls in too tight when working chart, go up a hook size or two. Do not pull yarns tight while working—it will cause puckering in the fabric and distortion of the pattern.

Instructions

With A, loosely ch 9.

Row 1 (RS): Work Foundation Row across.

Rows 2–61: With A, TKS in first st, with A and B, work Chart in TKS in each st across following Chart until 1 st remains. With A, work last st.

Fasten off B.

Row 62: With A, work TKS in each st across.

Bind off.

Fasten off.

Finishing

With yarn needle, weave in tails. Dampen headband, gently squeezing out excess water. Place headband on a padded ironing board. Place a wet towel on top of curling edge. Smooth the edge as flat as possible with your hand, making sure there are no lumps or wrinkles. Gently place the iron on top of the wet towel. Do not hold it in place for very long. Lift the iron and wet towel and move down the edge, repeating the process as you go across. When headband has been completely steam blocked, pin to blocking mat and allow to fully dry. Sew ends together.

Eliza Headband

 Color A

 Color B

Emily Headband

Emily brings class with a bit of sass to any winter outfit. The colors really pop! You will be a standout for sure in this lovely design.

Skill Level
Beginner

Finished Measurements
About 3$\frac{1}{2}$ in. (9 cm) wide x 21 in. (51 cm) long

Yarn
Caron® International Simply Soft® Heathers (100% acrylic; 5 oz./141.7 g;
  250 yd./228 m)
• 1 skein #9509 Grey Heather (A)
Caron® International Simply Soft® (100% acrylic; 6 oz./170.1 g;
  315 yd./288 m)
• 1 skein #0012 Passion (B)

Hook & Other Materials
• US H/8 (5 mm) Tunisian crochet cabled hook or size to obtain gauge
• Yarn needle
• Stitch markers

Gauge
In TKS 16 sts and 18 rows = 4 in. (10 cm)

Pattern Stitches

Foundation Row: Insert hook in second chain from hook, yarn over, pull up loop, *insert hook in next chain, yarn over, pull up loop; repeat from * across. Leave all loops on hook. Do not turn. **Return Pass:** Yarn over, pull through 1 loop on hook, *yarn over, pull through 2 loops on hook; repeat from * across until 1 loop remains. (See step-by-step instructions on page 3.)

Tunisian Purl Stitch (TPS): Skip first vertical bar, bring yarn in front of work,*insert hook under next vertical bar, yarn over, pull up loop; repeat from * across until 1 stitch remains, insert hook through both loops in end stitch, yarn over, pull loop up. Do not turn. **Return Pass:** Yarn over, pull through 1 loop, *yarn over, pull through 2 loops on hook; repeat from * across until 1 loop remains. (See step-by-step instructions on page 7.)

Tunisian Knit Stitch (TKS): Skip first vertical bar, *insert hook through next stitch from front to back between strands of vertical bar, yarn over, pull up loop; repeat from * across until 1 stitch remains, insert hook through both loops in end stitch, yarn over, pull loop up. Do not turn. **Return Pass:** Yarn over, pull through 1 loop on hook, *yarn over, pull through 2 loops on hook; repeat from * across until 1 loop remains. Do not turn. (See step-by-step instructions on page 5.)

Bind Off: Skip first vertical bar, *insert hook through next stitch from front to back between strands of vertical bar, yarn over, pull up loop, draw yarn through loop on hook; repeat from * across number of stitches indicated. (See step-by-step instructions on page 12.)

Notes

If gauge pulls in too tight when working chart, go up a hook size or two. Do not pull yarns tight while working—it will cause puckering in the fabric and distortion of the pattern.

Instructions

With A, loosely ch 84.

Row 1 (RS): Work Foundation Row across.

Rows 2–3: Work TPS in each st across.

Row 4: Work TKS in each st across.

Rows 5–11: With A and B, work Chart in TKS in each st across.

Fasten off B.

Row 12: With A, work TKS in each st across.

Rows 13–14: Work TPS each st across.

Bind off.

Fasten off.

Finishing

With yarn needle, weave in tails. Dampen headband, gently squeezing out excess water. Place headband on a padded ironing board. Place a wet towel on top of curling edge. Smooth the edge as flat as possible with your hand, making sure there are no lumps or wrinkles. Gently place the iron on top of the wet towel. Do not hold it in place for very long. Lift the iron and wet towel and move down the edge, repeating the process as you go across. When headband has been completely steam blocked, pin to blocking mat and allow to fully dry. Sew ends together.

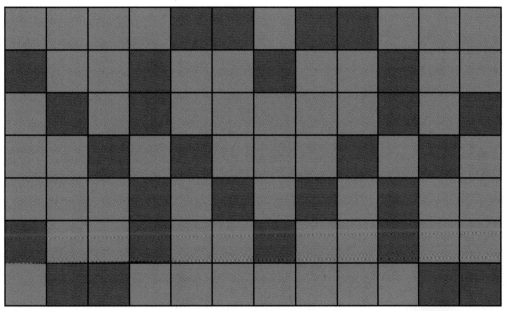

Emily Headband

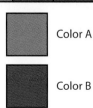

Color A

Color B

Sabela Cowl

Sabela is perfect for those long fall days when the chill of winter begins to creep in.

Skill Level
Advanced Beginner

Finished Measurements
About 7 in. (18 cm) wide x 26 in. (71 cm) long

Yarn
Berroco Comfort (50% nylon, 50% acrylic; 3.5 oz./100 g; 210 yd./193 m)
- 2 skeins #9717 Raspberry Coulis (A)
- 2 skeins #9720 Hummus (B)

Hook & Other Materials
- US I/9 (5.5 mm) Tunisian crochet cabled hook or size to obtain gauge
- Yarn needle
- Stitch markers

Gauge
In TKS 16 sts and 16 rows = 4 in. (10 cm)

Pattern Stitches

Foundation Row: Insert hook in second chain from hook, yarn over, pull up loop, *insert hook in next chain, yarn over, pull up loop; repeat from * across. Leave all loops on hook. Do not turn. **Return Pass:** Yarn over, pull through 1 loop on hook, *yarn over, pull through 2 loops on hook; repeat from * across until 1 loop remains. (See step-by-step instructions on page 3.)

Tunisian Purl Stitch (TPS): Skip first vertical bar, bring yarn in front of work, *insert hook under next vertical bar, yarn over, pull up loop; repeat from * across until 1 stitch remains, insert hook through both loops in end stitch, yarn over, pull loop up. Do not turn. **Return Pass:** Yarn over, pull through 1 loop, *yarn over, pull through 2 loops on hook; repeat from * across until 1 loop remains. (See step-by-step instructions on page 7.)

Tunisian Knit Stitch (TKS): Skip first vertical bar, *insert hook through next stitch from front to back between strands of vertical bar, yarn over, pull up loop; repeat from * across until 1 stitch remains, insert hook through both loops in end stitch, yarn over, pull loop up. Do not turn. **Return Pass:** Yarn over, pull through 1 loop on hook, *yarn over, pull through 2 loops on hook; repeat from * across until 1 loop remains. Do not turn. (See step-by-step instructions on page 5.)

Bind Off: Skip first vertical bar, *insert hook through next stitch from front to back between strands of vertical bar, yarn over, pull up loop, draw yarn through loop on hook; repeat from * across number of stitches indicated. (See step-by-step instructions on page 12.)

Notes

If gauge pulls in too tight when working chart, go up a hook size or two. Do not pull yarns tight while working—it will cause puckering in the fabric and distortion of the pattern.

Instructions

With A, loosely ch 105.

Row 1 (RS): Work Foundation Row across.

Row 2: Work TPS in each st across.

Row 3: With B, work TKS in each st across.

Row 4: With A, work TKS in each st across.

Row 5: With B, work TKS in each st across.

Rows 6–24: With A and B, work Chart in TKS in each st across.

Row 25: With B, work TKS in each st across.

Row 26: With A, work TKS in each st across.

Row 27: With B, work TKS in each st across.

Fasten off B.

Row 28: With A, work TPS in each st across.

Bind off.

Fasten off.

Finishing

With yarn needle, weave in tails. Dampen cowl, gently squeezing out excess water. Place cowl on a padded ironing board. Place a wet towel on top of curling edge. Smooth the edge as flat as possible with your hand, making sure there are no lumps or wrinkles. Gently place the iron on top of the wet towel. Do not hold it in place for very long. Lift the iron and wet towel and move down the edge, repeating the process as you go across. When cowl has been completely steam blocked, pin to blocking mat and allow to fully dry. Sew ends together.

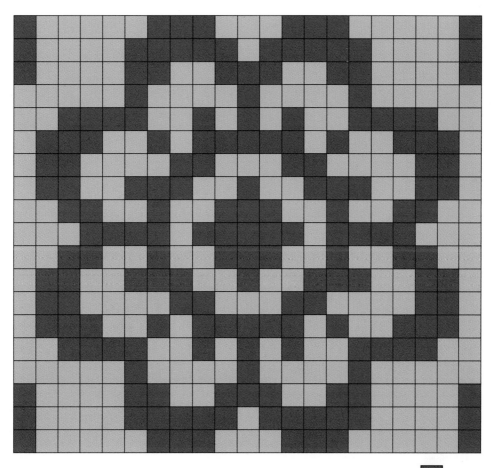

Sabela Cowl

Color A

Color B

Merryn Cowl

Merryn is a classical representation of the traditional Fair Isle snowflake.

The perfect addition to any winter outfit!

Skill Level
Advanced Beginner

Finished Measurements
About $8^1/_4$ in. (18 cm) wide x 25 in. (63.5 cm) long

Yarn
Universal Yarn Uptown DK (100% acrylic; 3.5 oz./100 g; 273 yd./250 m)
- 1 skein #112 Cedar (A)
- 1 skein #102 Lily (B)

Hook & Other Materials
- US I/9 (5.5 mm) Tunisian crochet cabled hook or size to obtain gauge
- Yarn needle
- Stitch markers

Gauge
In TKS 18 sts and 14 rows = 4 in. (10 cm)

Pattern Stitches

Foundation Row: Insert hook in second chain from hook, yarn over, pull up loop, *insert hook in next chain, yarn over, pull up loop; repeat from * across. Leave all loops on hook. Do not turn. **Return Pass:** Yarn over, pull through 1 loop on hook, *yarn over, pull through 2 loops on hook; repeat from * across until 1 loop remains. (See step-by-step instructions on page 3.)

Tunisian Purl Stitch (TPS): Skip first vertical bar, bring yarn in front of work, *insert hook under next vertical bar, yarn over, pull up loop; repeat from * across until 1 stitch remains, insert hook through both loops in end stitch, yarn over, pull loop up. Do not turn. **Return Pass:** Yarn over, pull through 1 loop, *yarn over, pull through 2 loops on hook; repeat from * across until 1 loop remains. (See step-by-step instructions on page 7.)

Tunisian Knit Stitch (TKS): Skip first vertical bar, *insert hook through next stitch from front to back between strands of vertical bar, yarn over, pull up loop; repeat from * across until 1 stitch remains, insert hook through both loops on end stitch, yarn over, pull loop up. Do not turn. **Return Pass:** Yarn over, pull through 1 loop on hook, *yarn over, pull through 2 loops on hook; repeat from * across until 1 loop remains. Do not turn. (See step-by-step instructions on page 5.)

Bind Off: Skip first vertical bar, *insert hook through next stitch from front to back between strands of vertical bar, yarn over, pull up loop, draw yarn through loop on hook; repeat from * across number of stitches indicated. (See step-by-step instructions on page 12.)

Notes

If gauge pulls in too tight when working chart, go up a hook size or two. Do not pull yarns tight while working—it will cause puckering in the fabric and distortion of the pattern.

Instructions

With A, loosely ch 112.

Row 1 (RS): Work Foundation Row across.

Rows 2–4: Work TPS in each st across.

Row 5: Work TKS in each st across.

Rows 6–24: With A and B, work Chart in TKS in each st across.

Fasten off color B.

Row 25: With A, work TKS in each st across.

Rows 26–28: Work TPS in each st across.

Bind off.

Fasten off.

Finishing

With yarn needle, weave in tails. Dampen cowl, gently squeezing out excess water. Place cowl on a padded ironing board. Place a wet towel on top of curling edge. Smooth the edge as flat as possible with your hand, making sure there are no lumps or wrinkles. Gently place the iron on top of the wet towel. Do not hold it in place for very long. Lift the iron and wet towel and move down the edge, repeating the process as you go across. When cowl has been completely steam blocked, pin to blocking mat and allow to fully dry. Sew ends together.

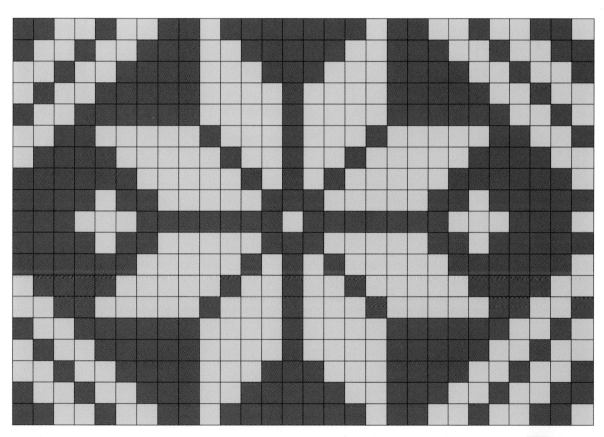

Merryn Cowl

■ Color A
□ Color B

Jelena Cowl

Jelena is sure to brighten any snowy winter day with these vibrant splashes of color.

Skill Level
Advanced Beginner

Finished Measurements
About $5^3/_4$ in. (14 cm) wide x $25^1/_2$ in. (66 cm) long

Yarn
Berroco Comfort (50% nylon, 50% acrylic; 3.50 oz./100 g; 210 yd./193 m)
* 1 skein #9736 Primary Blue (A)
* 1 skein #9743 Goldenrod (B)

Hook & Other Materials
* US 1/9 (5.5 mm) Tunisian crochet cabled hook or size to obtain gauge
* Yarn needle
* Stitch markers

Gauge
In TKS 16 sts and 16 rows = 4 in. (10 cm)

Pattern Stitches

Foundation Row: Insert hook in second chain from hook, yarn over, pull up loop, *insert hook in next chain, yarn over, pull up loop; repeat from * across. Leave all loops on hook. Do not turn. **Return Pass:** Yarn over, pull through 1 loop on hook, *yarn over, pull through 2 loops on hook; repeat from * across until 1 loop remains. (See step-by-step instructions on page 3.)

Tunisian Purl Stitch (TPS): Skip first vertical bar, bring yarn in front of work, *insert hook under next vertical bar, yarn over, pull up loop; repeat from * across until 1 stitch remains, insert hook through both loops in end stitch, yarn over, pull loop up. Do not turn. **Return Pass:** Yarn over, pull through 1 loop, *yarn over, pull through 2 loops on hook; repeat from * across until 1 loop remains. (See step-by-step instructions on page 7.)

Tunisian Knit Stitch (TKS): Skip first vertical bar, *insert hook through next stitch from front to back between strands of vertical bar, yarn over, pull up loop; repeat from * across until 1 stitch remains, insert hook through both loops in end stitch, yarn over, pull loop up. Do not turn. **Return Pass:** Yarn over, pull through 1 loop on hook, *yarn over, pull through 2 loops on hook; repeat from * across until 1 loop remains. Do not turn. (See step-by-step instructions on page 5.)

Bind Off: Skip first vertical bar, *insert hook through next stitch from front to back between strands of vertical bar, yarn over, pull up loop, draw yarn through loop on hook; repeat from * across number of stitches indicated. (See step-by-step instructions on page 12.)

Notes

If gauge pulls in too tight when working chart, go up a hook size or two. Do not pull yarns tight while working—it will cause puckering in the fabric and distortion of the pattern.

Instructions

With A, loosely ch 102.

Row 1 (RS): Work Foundation Row across.

Rows 2–3: Work TPS in each st across.

Row 4: Work TKS in each st across.

Rows 5–19: With A and B, work Chart in TKS in each st across.

Fasten off B.

Row 20: With A, work TKS in each st across.

Row 21–22: Work TPS in each st across.

Bind off.

Fasten off.

Finishing

With yarn needle, weave in tails. Dampen cowl, gently squeezing out excess water. Place cowl on a padded ironing board. Place a wet towel on top of curling edge. Smooth the edge as flat as possible with your hand, making sure there are no lumps or wrinkles. Gently place the iron on top of the wet towel. Do not hold it in place for very long. Lift the iron and wet towel and move down the edge, repeating the process as you go across. When cowl has been completely steam blocked, pin to blocking mat and allow to fully dry. Sew ends together.

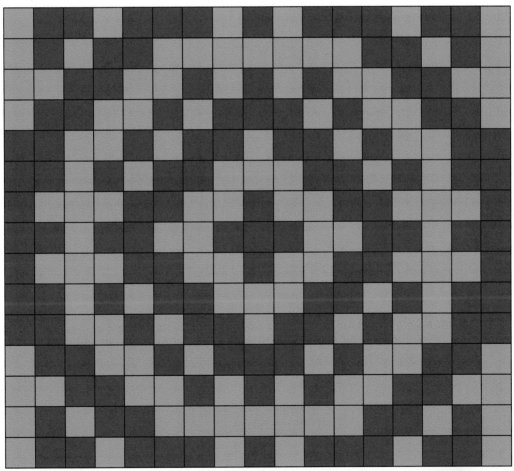

Jelena Cowl

Color A

Color B

Ivana Mitts

Ivana will take your Fair Isle Tunisian crochet to the next level with these fun and stylish multicolored mitts!

Skill Level
Intermediate

Finished Measurements
About 8 in. (20 cm) wide x 8 in. (20 cm) long

Yarn
Berroco Comfort (50% nylon, 50% acrylic; 3.5 oz./100 g; 210 yd./193 m)
- 2 skeins #9735 Delft Blue (A)
- 1 skein #9703 Barley (B)
- 1 skein #9717 Raspberry Coulis (C)

Hook & Other Materials
- US I/9 (5.5 mm) Tunisian crochet cabled hook or size to obtain gauge
- Yarn needle
- Stitch markers

Gauge
In TKS 14 sts and 14 rows = 4 in. (10 cm)

1 loop remains. (See step-by-step instructions on page 3.)

Tunisian Knit Stitch (TKS): Skip first vertical bar, *insert hook through next stitch from front to back between strands of vertical bar, yarn over, pull up loop; repeat from * across until 1 stitch remains, insert hook through both loops in end stitch, yarn over, pull loop up. Do not turn. **Return Pass:** Yarn over, pull through 1 loop on hook, *yarn over, pull through 2 loops on hook; repeat from * across until 1 loop remains. Do not turn. (See step-by-step instructions on page 5.)

Tunisian Purl Stitch (TPS): Skip first vertical bar, bring yarn in front of work, *insert hook under next vertical bar, yarn over, pull up loop; repeat from * across until 1 stitch remains, insert hook through both loops in end stitch, yarn over, pull loop up. Do not turn. **Return Pass:** Yarn over, pull through 1 loop, *yarn over, pull through 2 loops on hook; repeat from * across until 1 loop remains. (See step-by-step instructions on page 7.)

Bind Off: Skip first vertical bar, *insert hook through next stitch from front to back between strands of vertical bar, yarn over, pull up loop, draw yarn through loop on hook; repeat from * across number of stitches indicated. (See step-by-step instructions on page 12.)

Notes

- Bottom ribbing is made first; stitches are picked up on the edge of completed ribbing.
- If gauge pulls in too tight when working chart, go up a hook size or two. Do not pull yarns tight while working—it will cause puckering in the fabric and distortion of the pattern.

Instructions

Ribbing (make two)

With A, loosely ch 6.

Row 1: Sc in second ch from hook and in each st across. Turn.

Rows 2–28: Ch 1, blsc in each st across. Turn. Do not fasten off. Turn ribbing so you can pick up sts on the top for the body of the mitts.

Pattern Stitches

Single Crochet (sc): Insert hook where pattern instructs, yarn over, pull through loop, yarn over and pull through both loops. (See step-by-step instructions on page 16.)

Back Loop Single Crochet (blsc): Insert hook underneath the back loop only in stitch below, yarn over, pull through loop, yarn over, and pull through both loops. (See step-by-step instructions on page 16.)

Foundation Row: Insert hook in place indicated, yarn over, pull up loop, *insert hook in next space, yarn over, pull up loop; repeat from * across. Leave all loops on hook. Do not turn. **Return Pass:** Yarn over, pull through 1 loop on hook, *yarn over, pull through 2 loops on hook; repeat from * across until

Body (make two)

Row 1 (RS): With A, work Foundation Row, pulling up 28 loops along top of ribbing.

Rows 2–25: With A, B, and C, work Chart in TKS in each st across.

Fasten off colors B and C.

Row 26: With A, work TKS in each st across.

Rows 27–28: Work TPS in each st across.

Bind off.

Fasten off.

Finishing

With yarn needle, weave in tails. Dampen mitts and gently squeeze out excess water. Place mitts on a padded ironing board. Place a wet towel on top of curling edge. Smooth the edge as flat as possible with your hand, making sure there are no lumps or wrinkles. Gently place the iron on top of the wet towel. Do not hold it in place for very long. Lift the iron and wet towel and move down the edge, repeating the process as you go across. When mitts have been completely steam blocked, pin to blocking mat and allow to fully dry.

Sew 4 in. (10 cm) of side together from bottom, skip 1¹/₂ in. (4 cm) (thumb hole made), sew remaining side together, and weave in tails.

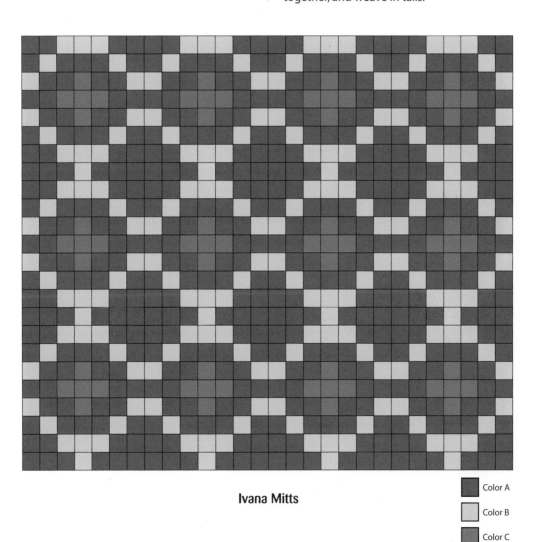

Ivana Mitts

Color A

Color B

Color C

Adisa Mitts

Adisa mitts are perfect for texting, web surfing, or crocheting! They keep your fingers free while your hands stay nice and toasty.

Skill Level
Advanced Beginner

Finished Measurements
About 8 in. (20 cm) wide x 8 in. (20 cm) long

Yarn
Lion Brand Heartland (100% acrylic; 5 oz./142 g; 251 yd./230 m)
- 1 skein #136-153 Black Canyon (A)
- 1 skein #136-103 Denali (B)

Hook & Other Materials
- US I/9 (5.5 mm) Tunisian crochet cabled hook or size to obtain gauge
- Yarn needle
- Stitch markers

Gauge
In TKS 16 sts and 16 rows = 4 in. (10 cm)

Pattern Stitches

Foundation Row: Insert hook in second chain from hook, yarn over, pull up loop, *insert hook in next chain, yarn over, pull up loop; repeat from * across. Leave all loops on hook. Do not turn. **Return Pass:** Yarn over, pull through 1 loop on hook, *yarn over, pull through 2 loops on hook; repeat from * across until 1 loop remains. (See step-by-step instructions on page 3.)

Tunisian Purl Stitch (TPS): Skip first vertical bar, bring yarn in front of work, *insert hook under next vertical bar, yarn over, pull up loop; repeat from * across until 1 stitch remains, insert hook through both loops in end stitch, yarn over, pull loop up. Do not turn. **Return Pass:** Yarn over, pull through 1 loop, *yarn over, pull through 2 loops on hook; repeat from * across until 1 loop remains. (See step-by-step instructions on page 7.)

Tunisian Knit Stitch (TKS): Skip first vertical bar, *insert hook through next stitch from front to back between strands of vertical bar, yarn over, pull up loop; repeat from * across until 1 stitch remains, insert hook through both loops in end stitch, yarn over, pull loop up. Do not turn. **Return Pass:** Yarn over, pull through 1 loop on hook, *yarn over, pull through 2 loops on hook; repeat from * across until 1 loop remains. Do not turn. (See step-by-step instructions on page 5.)

Bind Off: Skip first vertical bar, *insert hook through next stitch from front to back between strands of vertical bar, yarn over, pull up loop, draw yarn through loop on hook; repeat from * across number of stitches indicated. (See step-by-step instructions on page 12.)

Notes

If gauge pulls in too tight when working chart, go up a hook size or two. Do not pull yarns tight while working—it will cause puckering in the fabric and distortion of the pattern.

Instructions (make two)

With A, loosely ch 33.

Row 1 (RS): Work Foundation Row across.

Rows 2–3: Work TPS in each st across.

Row 4: Work TKS in each st across.

Rows 5–26: With A and B, work Chart in TKS in each st across.

Fasten off B.

Row 27: With A, work TKS in each st across.

Rows 28–29: Work TPS in each st across.

Bind off.

Fasten off.

Finishing

With yarn needle, weave in tails. Dampen mitts, gently squeezing out excess water. Place mitts on a padded ironing board. Place a wet towel on top of curling edge. Smooth the edge as flat as possible with your hand, making sure there are no lumps or wrinkles. Gently place the iron on top of the wet towel. Do not hold it in place for very long. Lift the iron and wet towel and move down the edge, repeating the process as you go across. When mitts have been completely steam blocked, pin to blocking mat and allow to fully dry.

Sew 4 in. (10 cm) of side together from bottom, skip 1 1/2 in. (4 cm) (thumb hole made), sew remaining side together, and weave in tails.

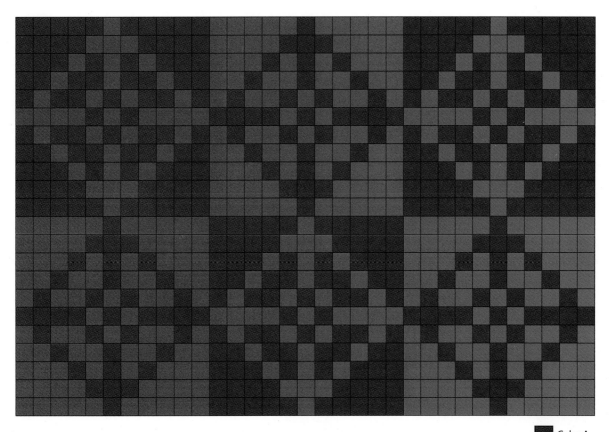

Adisa Mitts

Color A

Color B

Cora Sweater

Cora is a showstopper featuring a classically elegant structure with a colorful modern twist! This lovely sweater pairs great with jeans or a skirt. It's very easy to dress this top up or down depending on the occasion.

Skill Level
Advanced

Sizes
S (M, L, 1X, 2X, 3X)
Note: Instructions are given for smallest size; changes for larger sizes are given in parentheses. You may wish to circle all numbers that pertain to the desired size only.

Finished Measurements
Bust: 37 (41, 45, 49, 53, 57) in./94 (104, 114, 124.5, 135, 145) cm
Length: $20^1/_2$ ($21^1/_4$, 22, 23, 24, 24) in./52 (54, 56, 58, 61, 61) cm

Yarn
Cascade Yarns Avalon (50% acrylic, 50% cotton; 3.5 oz./100 g; 175 yd./160 m)
• 8 (9, 10, 11, 12, 13) skeins #22 Hyacinth Violet (A)
• 8 (9, 10, 11, 12, 13) skeins #21 Lilac Chiffon (B)

Hook & Other Materials
• US I/9 (5.5 mm) Tunisian crochet cabled hook or size to obtain gauge
• Clasp
• Yarn needle
• Stitch markers

Gauge
In TKS 15 sts and 15 rows = 4 in. (10 cm)

(Tunisian knit stitch made), with A, bring yarn in front of work, insert hook under next vertical bar, yarn over, pull up loop (Tunisian purl stitch made); repeat from * across until 1 stitch remains, insert hook through both loops in end stitch, yarn over, pull loop up. Do not turn. Work **Return Pass** in colors as they are presented: Yarn over, pull through 1 loop on hook, *yarn over, pull through 2 loops on hook; repeat from * across until 1 loop remains. Do not turn. Repeat Row 2 for pattern. (See step-by-step instructions on page 14.)

Tunisian Knit Stitch (TKS): Skip first vertical bar, *insert hook through next stitch from front to back between strands of vertical bar, yarn over, pull up loop; repeat from * across until 1 stitch remains, insert hook through both loops in end stitch, yarn over, pull loop up. Do not turn. **Return Pass:** Yarn over, pull through 1 loop on hook, *yarn over, pull through 2 loops on hook; repeat from * across until 1 loop remains. Do not turn. (See step-by-step instructions on page 5.)

Tunisian Purl Stitch (TPS): Skip first vertical bar, bring yarn in front of work, *insert hook under next vertical bar, yarn over, pull up loop; repeat from * across until 1 stitch remains, insert hook through both loops in end stitch, yarn over, pull loop up. Do not turn. **Return Pass:** Yarn over, pull through 1 loop, *yarn over, pull through 2 loops on hook; repeat from * across until 1 loop remains. (See step-by-step instructions on page 7.)

Bind Off: Skip first vertical bar, *insert hook through next stitch from front to back between strands of vertical bar, yarn over, pull up loop, draw yarn through loop on hook; repeat from * across number of stitches indicated. (See step-by-step instructions on page 12.)

Tunisian Increase Stitch: Insert hook between stitches indicated, yarn over, pull up loop, increase made. (See step-by-step instructions on page 9.)

Notes

- Body is made in one piece, worked from the bottom ribbing up to the armholes. The two front panels and back panel are then worked separately and seamed at the shoulder. Sleeves are then made one at a time and sewn into armhole openings. The

Pattern Stitches

Ribbing Row 1: Pull up loop in color B, pull up next loop in color A; repeat across. **Return Pass** in color as presented: Yarn over, pull through 1 loop on hook, *yarn over, pull through 2 loops on hook; repeat from * across until 1 loop remains. Do not turn. (See step-by-step instructions on page 13.)

Ribbing Row 2: Skip first vertical bar, *insert hook through next stitch from front to back between strands of vertical bar, with B, yarn over, pull up loop

ribbing around the neck is worked next, and then the ribbing for each front panel is worked.

- The last repeat is only 13 stitches of the chart on all sizes.
- Sleeves are designed to hit midway between the wrist and elbow.
- If gauge pulls in too tight when working the chart, go up a hook size or two. Do not pull yarns tight while working—it will cause puckering in the fabric and distortion of the pattern.

Instructions

With A, loosely ch 139 (153, 167, 181, 195, 209).

Row 1 (RS): Work Ribbing Row 1 across.

Rows 2–4: With A and B, work Ribbing Row 2 in each st across.

With A and B, work Chart in TKS in each st across until piece measures 13 (13^1/$_2$, 14, 14^1/$_2$, 15, 15) in./33 (34, 35.5, 37, 38, 38) cm.

(continued)

Cora Sweater

Color A

Color B

Right Front Panel

With A and B, work Chart in TKS in 29 (33, 37, 41, 45, 49) sts on right front side (armhole shaping made). Continue working in Chart for $6^1/_4$ ($6^1/_2$, $6^3/_4$, $7^3/_4$, $8^3/_4$, $8^3/_4$) in./16 (16.5, 17, 20, 22, 22) cm.

Right Front Neck Shaping

When piece measures $6^1/_4$ ($6^1/_2$, $6^3/_4$, $7^3/_4$, $8^3/_4$, $8^3/_4$) in./16 (16.5, 17, 20, 22, 22) cm, * bind off each of the next 3 (3, 4, 6, 8, 10) sts, work Chart in TKS in each remaining st; repeat from * 2 more times, work Chart in TKS in each remaining st. Bind off remaining sts. Fasten off.

Back Shaping

Skip 12 (13, 14, 15, 16, 17) sts from right front for armhole, work Chart in TKS across 57 (61, 65, 69, 73, 77) sts. Continue working in Chart for $7^1/_2$ ($7^3/_4$, 8, $8^1/_2$, 9, 9) in./19 (19.5, 20, 21.5, 23, 23) cm. Bind off. Fasten off.

Left Front Panel

Skip 12 (13, 14, 15, 16, 17) sts from back for armhole, work Chart in TKS in each remaining 29 (33, 37, 41, 45, 49) sts. Continue working in Chart for $6^1/_4$ ($6^1/_2$, $6^3/_4$, $7^3/_4$, $8^3/_4$, $8^3/_4$) in./16 (16.5, 17, 20, 22, 22) cm. Begin left neck shaping.

Left Front Neck Shaping

When piece measures $6^1/_4$ ($6^1/_2$, $6^3/_4$, $7^3/_4$, $8^3/_4$, $8^3/_4$) in./16 (16.5, 17, 20, 22, 22) cm, *TKS across in Chart leaving the last 3 (3, 4, 6, 8, 10) sts unworked; repeat from * 2 more times. Bind off remaining sts. Fasten off.

Sleeves (make two)

With A, loosely ch 42 (46, 48, 50, 52, 54).

Row 1 (RS): With A and B, work Ribbing Row 1, pulling up loops evenly across.

Rows 2–4: With A and B, work Ribbing Row 2 across.

Begin working sleeve in Chart. Work Tunisian increase stitch between first 2 sts and last 2 sts every other row (2 increases made per increase row) until you have 58 (62, 64, 66, 68, 70) sts. Work until sleeve measures 11 ($11^1/_4$, 12, $12^1/_2$, 13, 13) in./28 (28.5, 30.5, 32, 33, 33) cm from the beginning. Begin the bind off.

Bind off 1 st at the beginning and leave 1 st unworked at the end of every row until 28 (32, 36, 38, 42, 46) sts remain. Bind off 1 st at the beginning and leave 1 st unworked, work 3 more rows, bind off 1 st at the beginning and leave 1 st unworked at the end of every row until 6 (8, 10, 12, 14, 16) sts remain. Fasten off. Cap sleeve made.

Finishing

With yarn needle, weave in tails. Dampen all sweater pieces, gently squeezing out excess water. Place pieces on a padded ironing board. Place a wet towel on top of curling edge. Smooth the edge as flat as possible with your hand, making sure there are no lumps or wrinkles. Gently place the iron on top of the wet towel. Do not hold it in place for very long. Lift the iron and wet towel and move down the edge, repeating the process as you go across. When pieces have been completely steam blocked, pin to blocking mat and allow to fully dry.

Sew shoulder seams. Sew in sleeves. Sew sleeve side seams. Add neck and front ribbing, as below.

Neck Ribbing

Row 1 (RS): Working from right to left in neck opening, with A and B, work Ribbing Row 1, pulling up 50 loops evenly around.

Rows 2–4: With A and B, work Ribbing Row 2 across. Fasten off.

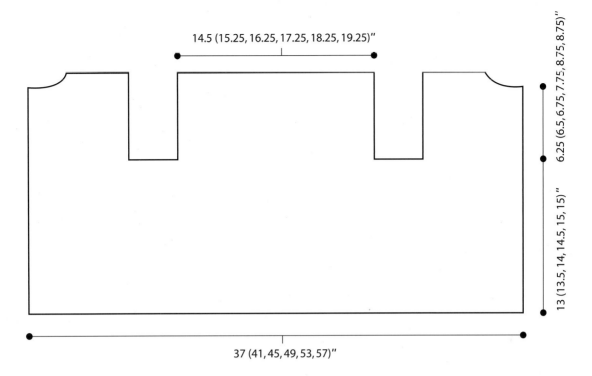

14.5 (15.25, 16.25, 17.25, 18.25, 19.25)"

6.25 (6.5, 6.75, 7.75, 8.75, 8.75)"

13 (13.5, 14, 14.5, 15, 15)"

37 (41, 45, 49, 53, 57)"

Finished Measurements—Body

Right Front Ribbing

Row 1 (RS): Working from bottom to top of right cardigan front opening, with A and B, work Ribbing Row 1, pulling up 93 (96, 99, 103, 107, 107) loops total (including pulling up loops on side of neck ribbing).

Rows 2–4: With A and B, work Ribbing Row 2 in each st across. Fasten off.

Left Front Ribbing

Row 1 (RS): Working from bottom to top of left cardigan front opening, with A and B, work Ribbing Row 1, pulling up 93 (96, 99, 103, 107, 107) loops total (including pulling up loops on side of neck ribbing).

Rows 2–4: With A and B, work Ribbing Row 2 in each st across. Fasten off.

Block again, if desired.

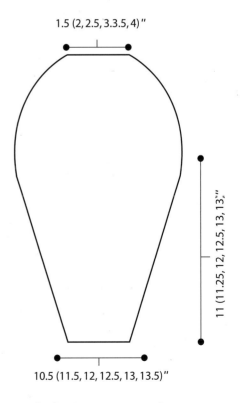

1.5 (2, 2.5, 3.3.5, 4)"

11 (11.25, 12, 12.5, 13, 13)"

10.5 (11.5, 12, 12.5, 13, 13.5)"

Finished Measurements—Sleeve

Laleh Sweater

Laleh is truly the perfect ski sweater! The bright pink and blue will really stand out against the snow, and the thickness of the fabric is sure to keep you warm and toasty when you hit the slopes!

Skill Level
Advanced

Sizes
S (M, L, 1X, 2X, 3X)
Note: Instructions are given for smallest size; changes for larger sizes are given in parentheses. You may wish to circle all numbers that pertain to the desired size only.

Finished Measurements
Bust: 37^1/$_2$ (41^1/$_2$, 45^1/$_2$, 49^1/$_2$, 53^1/$_2$, 57^1/$_2$) in./95 (105, 115.5, 126, 136, 146) cm
Length: 24 (24^1/$_2$, 25, 25, 25^1/$_2$, 26) in./61 (62, 63.5, 63.5, 65, 66) cm

Yarn
Cascade Yarns Cherub DK (45% acrylic, 55% nylon; 1.75 oz./50 g;
    180 yd./165 m)
- 10 (11, 12, 13, 14, 15) skeins #45 Raspberry (A)
- 5 (6, 7, 8, 9, 9) skeins #34 Classic Blue (B)

Hook & Other Materials
- US H/8 (5 mm) Tunisian crochet cabled hook or size to obtain gauge
- Yarn needle
- Stitch markers

Gauge
In TKS 16 sts and 16 rows = 4 in. (10 cm)

Pattern Stitches

Foundation Row: Insert hook in second chain from hook, yarn over, pull up loop, *insert hook in next chain, yarn over, pull up loop; repeat from * across. Leave all loops on hook. Do not turn. **Return Pass:** Yarn over, pull through 1 loop on hook, *yarn over, pull through 2 loops on hook; repeat from * across until 1 loop remains. (See step-by-step instructions on page 3.)

Tunisian Knit Stitch (TKS): Skip first vertical bar, *insert hook through next stitch from front to back between strands of vertical bar, yarn over, pull up loop; repeat from * across until 1 stitch remains, insert hook through both loops in end stitch, yarn over, pull loop up. Do not turn. **Return Pass:** Yarn over, pull through 1 loop on hook, *yarn over, pull through 2 loops on hook; repeat from * across until 1 loop remains. Do not turn. (See step-by-step instructions on page 5.)

Tunisian Purl Stitch (TPS): Skip first vertical bar, bring yarn in front of work, *insert hook under next vertical bar, yarn over, pull up loop; repeat from * across until 1 stitch remains, insert hook through both loops in end stitch, yarn over, pull loop up. Do not turn. **Return Pass:** Yarn over, pull through 1 loop, *yarn over, pull through 2 loops on hook; repeat from * across until 1 loop remains. (See step-by-step instructions on page 7.)

Tunisian Seed Stitch (multiple of 2 stitches): Repeat Rows 1 and 2 for Tunisian seed stitch.

Row 1: Skip first vertical bar, *Tunisian knit stitch in next stitch, Tunisian purl stitch in next stitch; repeat from * across until 1 stitch remains, insert hook through both loops in end stitch, yarn over, pull loop up. Do not turn. **Return Pass:** Yarn over, pull through 1 loop on hook, *yarn over, pull through 2 loops on hook; repeat from * across until 1 loop remains. Do not turn.

Row 2: Skip first vertical bar, *Tunisian purl stitch in next stitch, Tunisian knit stitch in next stitch; repeat from * across until 1 stitch remains, insert hook through both loops in end stitch, yarn over, pull loop up. Do not turn. **Return Pass:** Yarn over, pull through 1 loop on hook, *yarn over, pull through 2 loops on hook; repeat from * across until 1 loop remains. Do not turn. (See step-by-step instructions on pages 9–12.)

Bind Off: Skip first vertical bar, *insert hook through next stitch from front to back between strands of vertical bar, yarn over, pull up loop, draw yarn through loop on hook; repeat from * across number of stitches indicated. (See step-by-step instructions on page 12.)

Tunisian Increase Stitch: Insert hook between stitches indicated, yarn over, pull up loop, increase made. (See step-by-step instructions on page 9.)

Notes

If gauge pulls in too tight when working chart, go up a hook size or two. Do not pull yarns tight while working—it will cause puckering in the fabric and distortion of the pattern.

Instructions

Back

With A, loosely ch 75 (83, 91, 99, 107, 115).

Row 1 (RS): Work Foundation Row across.

Rows 2–6: Work in Tunisian seed stitch in each stitch across.

Row 7: Work in TKS in each stitch across.

Continue working in TKS until piece measures $12^1/_2$ $(13, 13^1/_2, 13^1/_2, 14, 14^1/_2)$ in./32 (33, 34, 34, 35.5, 37) cm from beginning. Work one row in B. With A and B, begin working Chart in TKS. Continue working in Chart until body measures $14^1/_2$ (15, 15, 15, 15, 15) in./37 (38, 38, 38, 38, 38) cm from beginning.

(continued)

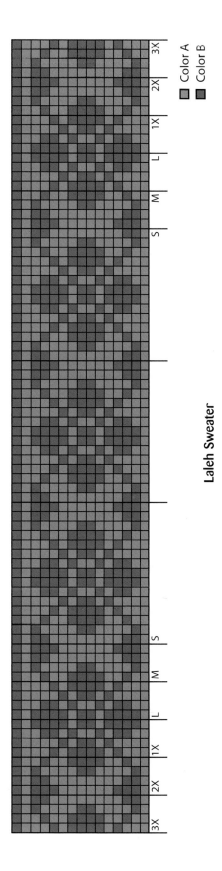

■ Color A
■ Color B

Laleh Sweater

Shape Armholes

When body measures 14$\frac{1}{2}$ (15, 15, 15, 15, 15) in./ 37 (38, 38, 38, 38, 38) cm from beginning, bind off first 7 (8, 10, 12, 14, 17) sts and work Chart in TKS in each st across, leaving last 7 (8, 10, 12, 14, 17) sts unworked. Continue working Chart in TKS for 6$\frac{1}{2}$ (6$\frac{1}{2}$, 7, 7, 7$\frac{1}{2}$, 8) in./16.5 (16.5, 18, 18, 19, 20) cm. Begin shoulder shaping.

Right Shoulder

Work Chart in TKS across first 16 (18, 19, 20, 22, 23) sts. Work until piece measures 23 (23$\frac{1}{2}$, 24, 24, 24$\frac{1}{2}$, 25) in./58.5 (60, 61, 61, 62, 63.5) cm from beginning. Bind off and fasten off.

Left Shoulder

Skip next 29 (31, 33, 35, 35, 35) unworked sts following first row of right shoulder and join yarn. Work Chart in TKS in next 16 (18, 19, 20, 22, 23) sts, working out to the edge. Work until piece measures 23 (23$\frac{1}{2}$, 24, 24, 24$\frac{1}{2}$, 25) in./58.5 (60, 61, 61, 62, 63.5) cm from beginning. Bind off and fasten off.

Front

With A, loosely ch 75 (83, 91, 99, 107, 115).
Row 1 (RS): Work Foundation Row across.
Rows 2–6: Work in Tunisian seed stitch in each st across.
Row 7: Work in TKS in each st across.
Continue working in TKS until piece measures 12$\frac{1}{2}$ (13, 13$\frac{1}{2}$, 13$\frac{1}{2}$, 14, 14$\frac{1}{2}$) in./32 (33, 34, 34, 35.5, 37) cm from beginning. Work one row in B. With A and B, work Chart in TKS. Continue working in Chart until body measures 14$\frac{1}{2}$ (15, 15, 15, 15, 15) in./37 (38, 38, 38, 38, 38) cm from beginning.

Shape Armholes

When body measures 14$\frac{1}{2}$ (15, 15, 15, 15, 15) in./37 (38, 38, 38, 38, 38) cm from beginning, bind off first 7 (8, 10, 12, 14, 17) sts, work Chart in TKS, leaving last 7 (8, 10, 12, 14, 17) sts unworked. Continue working Chart in TKS for 6$\frac{1}{2}$ (6$\frac{1}{2}$, 7, 7, 7$\frac{1}{2}$, 8) in./16.5 (16.5, 18, 18, 19, 20) cm. Begin shoulder shaping.

Right Shoulder

Work Chart in TKS across first 16 (18, 19, 20, 22, 23) sts. Work until piece measures 23 (23$\frac{1}{2}$, 24, 24, 24$\frac{1}{2}$, 25) in./58.5 (60, 61, 61, 62, 63.5) cm from beginning. Bind off and fasten off.

Left Shoulder

Skip next 29 (31, 33, 35, 35, 35) unworked sts following first row of right shoulder and join yarn. Work Chart in TKS each of next 16 (18, 19, 20, 22, 23) sts, working out to the edge. Work until piece measures 23 (23$\frac{1}{2}$, 24, 24, 24$\frac{1}{2}$, 25) in./58.5 (60, 61, 61, 62, 63.5) cm from beginning. Bind off and fasten off.

Sleeves (make two)

With A, loosely ch 41 (41, 49, 49, 49, 49).
Row 1 (RS): Work Foundation Row across.
Rows 2–6: Work in Tunisian seed stitch in each st across.
Rows 7–9: Work in TKS in each st across.
Row 10: Work in TKS across, making a Tunisian increase stitch in between the first and last st.
Continue working in TKS, making a Tunisian increase stitch in between the first and last st of every 4th row until there are 76 (80, 84, 84, 88, 88) sts total. Work until piece measures 21$\frac{1}{2}$ in./55 cm from beginning. Bind off and fasten off.

Finishing

Weave in tails. Dampen all sweater pieces, gently squeezing out excess water. Place pieces on a padded ironing board. Place a wet towel on top of the curling edge. Smooth the edge as flat as possible with your hand, making sure there are no lumps or wrinkles. Gently place the iron on top of the wet towel. Do not hold it in place for very long. Lift the iron and wet towel and move down the edge, repeating the process as you go across. When pieces have been completely steam blocked, pin to a blocking mat and allow to fully dry.

Sew shoulders together. Sew sleeves in arm openings. Sew sleeve seams and body seams. Weave in tails. Work neckband.

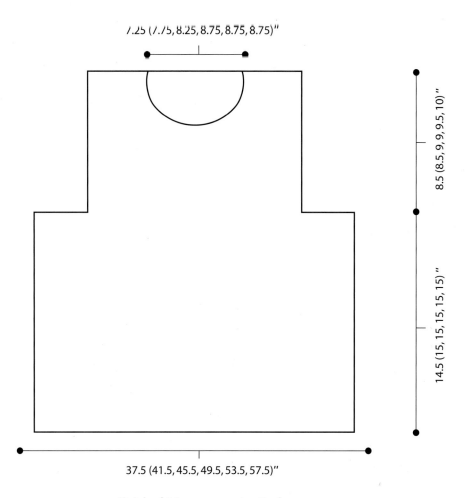

7.25 (7.75, 8.25, 8.75, 8.75, 8.75)"

8.5 (8.5, 9, 9, 9.5, 10)"

14.5 (15, 15, 15, 15, 15)"

37.5 (41.5, 45.5, 49.5, 53.5, 57.5)"

Finished Measurements–Body

Neckband

With RS facing, join A at center back and pull up 58 (62, 66, 70, 70, 70) loops.

Row 1: Work Foundation Row.

Rows 2–5: Work in Tunisian seed stitch in each st across. Bind off and fasten off.

Sew ends of neckband together and weave in tails. Block as necessary.

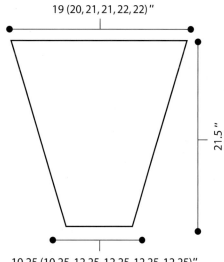

19 (20, 21, 21, 22, 22)"

21.5"

10.25 (10.25, 12.25, 12.25, 12.25, 12.25)"

Finished Measurements–Sleeve

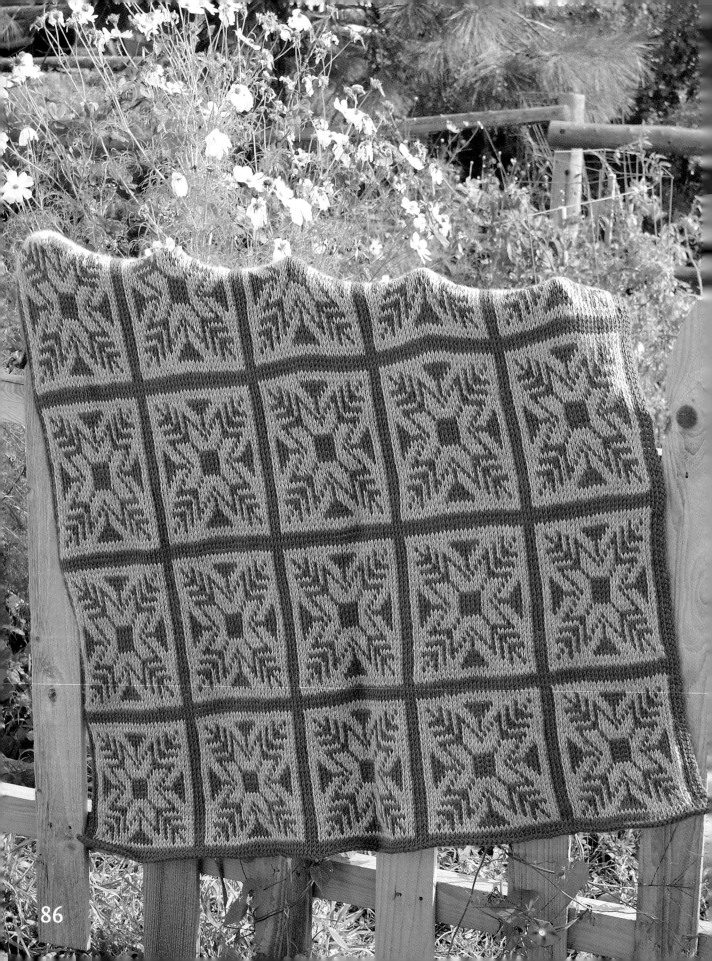

Elisha Afghan

Elisha brings tradition and elegance to life in one stunning afghan!

Skill Level
Intermediate

Finished Measurements
About 41 in. (96 cm) wide x 41 in. (112) cm long

Yarn
Red Heart Soft (100% acrylic; 5 oz./141 g; 256 yd./234 m)
- 7 skeins #9518 Teal (A)
- 7 skeins #9440 Light Grey Heather (B)

Hook & Other Materials
- US I/9 (5.5 mm) Tunisian crochet cabled hook or size to obtain gauge
- Yarn needle
- Stitch markers

Gauge
In TKS 16 sts and 16 rows = 4 in. (10 cm)

Pattern Stitches

Foundation Row: Insert hook in second chain from hook, yarn over, pull up loop, *insert hook in next chain, yarn over, pull up loop; repeat from * across. Leave all loops on hook. Do not turn. **Return Pass:** Yarn over, pull through 1 loop on hook, *yarn over, pull through 2 loops on hook; repeat from * across until 1 loop remains. (See step-by-step instructions on page 3.)

Tunisian Knit Stitch (TKS): Skip first vertical bar, *insert hook through next stitch from front to back between strands of vertical bar, yarn over, pull up loop; repeat from * across until 1 stitch remains, insert hook through both loops in end stitch, yarn over, pull loop up. Do not turn. **Return Pass:** Yarn over, pull through 1 loop on hook, *yarn over, pull through 2 loops on hook; repeat from * across until 1 loop remains. Do not turn. (See step-by-step instructions on page 5.)

Notes

If gauge pulls in too tight when working chart, go up a hook size or two. Do not pull yarns tight while working—it will cause puckering in the fabric and distortion of the pattern.

Instructions

With A, loosely ch 163.

Row 1 (RS): Work Foundation Row across.

Rows 2–3: Work TKS in each st across.

Rows 4–32: With A, TKS in each of next 3 sts, *with A and B, work Chart in TKS, with A, TKS in each of the next 3 sts; repeat from * across.

Rows 33–35: With A, work TKS in each st across.

Rows 36–163: Repeat Rows 4–35 four more times. Fasten off.

Finishing

With yarn needle, weave in tails. Dampen afghan, gently squeezing out excess water. Place afghan on a padded ironing board. Place a wet towel on top of curling edge. Smooth the edge as flat as possible with your hand, making sure there are no lumps or wrinkles. Gently place the iron on top of the wet towel. Do not hold it in place for very long. Lift the iron and wet towel and move down the edge, repeating the process as you go across. When afghan has been completely steam blocked, pin to blocking mat and allow to fully dry.

Elisha Afghan

■ Color A
■ Color B

Emma Afghan

Emma is a colorful explosion of all Fair Isle Tunisian crochet can be! The stark contrast of berry and cream make this afghan an all-time favorite!

Skill Level
Intermediate

Finished Measurements
About 37 in. (91 cm) wide x $36^1/_2$ in. (112 cm) long.

Yarn
Red Heart Soft (100% acrylic; 5 oz./141 g; 256 yd./234 m)
- 7 skeins #9979 Berry (A)
- 7 skeins #4601 Off White (B)

Hook & Other Materials
- US I/9 (5.5 mm) Tunisian crochet cabled hook or size to obtain gauge
- Yarn needle
- Stitch markers

Gauge
In TKS 18 stitches and 16 rows = 4 in. (10 cm)

Pattern Stitches

Foundation Row: Insert hook in second chain from hook, yarn over, pull up loop, *insert hook in next chain, yarn over, pull up loop; repeat from * across. Leave all loops on hook. Do not turn. **Return Pass:** Yarn over, pull through 1 loop on hook, *yarn over, pull through 2 loops on hook; repeat from * across until 1 loop remains. (See step-by-step instructions on page 3.)

Tunisian Knit Stitch (TKS): Skip first vertical bar, *insert hook through next stitch from front to back between strands of vertical bar, yarn over, pull up loop; repeat from * across until 1 stitch remains, insert hook through both loops in end stitch, yarn over, pull loop up. Do not turn. **Return Pass:** Yarn over, pull through 1 loop on hook, *yarn over, pull through 2 loops on hook; repeat from * across until 1 loop remains. Do not turn. (See step-by-step instructions on page 5.)

Notes

If gauge pulls in too tight when working chart, go up a hook size or two. Do not pull yarns tight while working—it will cause puckering in the fabric and distortion of the pattern.

Instructions

With A, loosely ch 167.
Row 1 (RS): Work Foundation Row across.

Rows 2–3: Work TKS in each st across.

Rows 4–16: With A, TKS in each of next 3 sts, with A and B, work Chart in TKS in each st across, with A, TKS in each of last 3 sts.

Row 17: With A, work TKS in each st across.

Row 18: With A, TKS in each of next 3 sts, *with B, TKS in next st, with A, TKS in next st; repeat from * until 3 sts remain, with A, TKS in each of last 3 sts.

Row 19: With A, work TKS in each st across.

Rows 20–163: Repeat Rows 4–19 nine more times. Fasten off B.

Rows 164–165: With A, work TKS in each st across. Fasten off.

Finishing

With yarn needle, weave in tails. Dampen afghan, gently squeezing out excess water. Place afghan on a padded ironing board. Place a wet towel on top of curling edge. Smooth the edge as flat as possible with your hand, making sure there are no lumps or wrinkles. Gently place the iron on top of the wet towel. Do not hold it in place for very long. Lift the iron and wet towel and move down the edge, repeating the process as you go across. When afghan has been completely steam blocked, pin to blocking mat and allow to fully dry.

Emma Afghan

■ Color A

☐ Color B

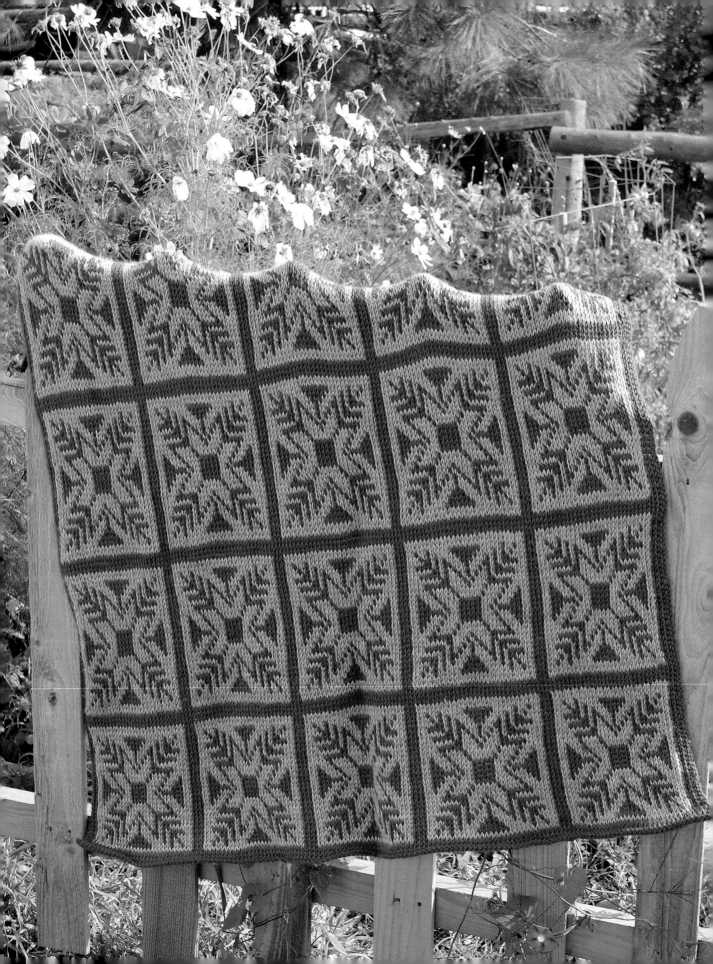

Suppliers

I would like to thank these yarn companies for their yarn support for my book. There are many others who generously donated yarn for swatching. Without them there would be no swatching or project yarns for designers to use in their samples. It is with deep gratitude I offer a very heartfelt thank you!

BERROCO, INC.
Comfort
1 Tupperware Dr., Suite 4
N. Smithfield, RI 02896
www.berroco.com

UNIVERSAL YARNS
Bamboo Pop, Uptown DK
5991 Caldwell Business Park Drive
Harrisburg, NC 28075
www.universalyarn.com

COATS AND CLARK
Red Heart Super Saver, Red Heart Boutique
Unforgettable, Red Heart Soft
P.O. Box 12229
Greenville, SC 29612
www.coatsandclark.com

LION BRAND
Vanna's Choice, Heartland
135 Kero Rd.
Carlstadt, NJ 07072
www.lionbrand.com

CARON® INTERNATIONAL/YARNSPIRATIONS
Simply Soft®
320 Livingstone Avenue South, Box 40
Listowel, ON Canada N4W 3H3
www.yarnspirations.com

CASCADE YARNS
Avalon, Cherub DK
1224 Andover Park E.
Tukwila, WA 98188
www.cascadeyarns.com

About the Photo-Shoot Location

I can't let this opportunity to introduce you to the state I love so much pass by. For twelve years my boys and I traveled all over, including moving overseas, following my husband as he served in the United States Air Force. We visited or lived in over forty different states and two foreign countries. They were beautiful and each held its own particular charm, but nothing compared to home—the Colorado Rocky Mountains.

Today we are so blessed to live seventy-five miles from the town we grew up in. Our sons are finally able to spend time with our families and explore all the glories the Colorado Rockies have to offer. My own ancestors were early pioneer settlers. Many of them were homesteaders who came from Ireland and staked their claims in the Dakotas and Wyoming. A few even made it to Colorado. Those people and places hold a very special place in my heart.

Clear Creek History Park is where the photos for this book were taken. It's a lovely little park nestled in downtown Golden, Colorado. Golden is tucked away in the foothills of the Colorado Rocky Mountains. This beautiful little park has so much history to offer! From root cellars to outhouses, it gives you a real appreciation for those who heeded the call to head west. Their bravery and tenacity are what paved the way for those of us enjoying the Rockies today. They had the foresight to preserve our heritage—something for which my family is greatly indebted to them.

Clear Creek History Park contains many of the original buildings from the Pearce Ranch in the Golden Gate Canyon. The buildings were carefully moved and preserved in the early 1990s when a housing development threatened to overtake them.

The gardens you see in the background are the Community Heirloom Gardens. These gardens are all grown from seed stock that was used by pioneer families over one hundred years ago. They are enchantingly beautiful and help feed the bees that are so lovingly tended to in this park.

The charming little one-room Guy Hill Schoolhouse was built in 1876 and was used as a school until 1951. Not only was it a school, but it was also used for community events and gatherings.

One of the cabins we photographed was the Pearce/Helps Cabin. This cabin is an original pioneer dwelling that dates back to at least 1878. William John and Susie Pearce are believed to have purchased the home in 1919, and they raised all four of their children there. The cabin was all hand-tooled and has dovetail notching on the corners—it's a true wonder to behold.

The second cabin we photographed was the Reynolds Cabin. This cabin is believed to have been built in 1873 and was owned by Adam and Annie Reynolds. They were neighbors of the Pearce family. In time this home and its 240-acre ranch was purchased by the Pearce family. Today it is used to hold educational programs.

We also used the blacksmith shop as a backdrop, as well as wagons, barrels, and authentic log rail fences. This area is, without a doubt, richly steeped in historical grandeur. Set in the awe-inspiring Rocky Mountains, it's really hard not to get lost in the romance of it all. It's also almost impossible to take a bad photo!

About the Author

___

Brenda Bourg is a knit and crochet designer, as well as a writer, teacher, and editor. Her designs have been published by *Knit 1-2-3*, *Cast On*, *Crochet 1-2-3*, *Crochet!*, *Crochet World*, Coats & Clark, Caron Yarns, SOHO, and Knit Picks. She is also co-editor of *Annie's Talking Crochet Newsletter*. You can even find her blogging occasionally at http://brendabourg.blogspot.com/. If it's fiber related, she can obsess over it pretty easily and write or talk about it for hours. She lives with her very understanding—and often enabling—husband, Robert, in Frederick, Colorado. Life is grand, and she is blessed!

Visual Index

Reena Headband 43

Eliza Headband 47

Emily Headband 51

Sabela Cowl 55

Merryn Cowl 59

Jelena Cowl 63

Ivana Mitts 67

Adisa Mitts 71

Cora Sweater 75

Laleh Sweater 81

Elisha Afghan 87

Emma Afghan 91